D0598413

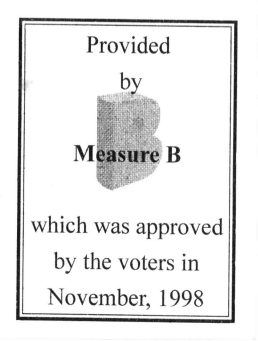

Provided

by

Measure B

which was approved

by the voters in

November, 1998

Depression

What You Need to Know

Margaret O. Hyde and
Elizabeth H. Forsyth, M.D.

Franklin Watts
A Division of Scholastic Inc.
New York • Toronto • London • Auckland
Sydney • Mexico City • New Delhi • Hong Kong
Danbury, Connecticut

Cover Design by Denis Folz
Interior Design by Kathleen Santini

Photographs ©: Photographs 2002: AP/Wide World Photos : 65
top; Corbis Images: 18, 19, 65 bottom (Bettmann), 72 (Corcoran
Gallery of Art), 8 (S.I.N.); Hulton l Archive/Getty Images: 71
(Baron), 20 (Hans Casparius), 16, 17, 74, 76; Jerry Bauer: 58;
Photo Researchers, NY/ Dr. P. Marazzi/SPL: 11; PhotoEdit: 59
(Tony Freeman), 10 left (Spencer Grant), 10 right, 84 (Michael
Newman), 57 (Mary Steinbacher), 68 (Rudi Von Briel), 13, 62
(David Young-Wolff); Stock Boston/ Dorothy Littell Greco: 36.

Chart on page 26 by Kathleen Santini

Library of Congress Cataloging-in-Publication Data

Hyde, Margaret O.
    Depression : what you need to know / Margaret O. Hyde
and Elizabeth H. Forsyth.
        p. cm.
Summary: Discusses the causes and symptoms of depression,
who suffers from this condition, and how it can be treated.
Includes bibliographical references and index.
    ISBN 0-531-11892-4
1. Depression in adolescence--Juvenile literature. 2. Depression,
Mental--Juvenile literature. 3. Teenagers--Suicidal behavior--
Prevention--Juvenile literature. [1. Depression, Mental.] I.
Forsyth, Elizabeth H. II. Title.
    RJ506.D4 H94 2002
    616.85'27--dc21

                                        2002002488

TABLE OF CONTENTS

Chapter One

THE BLACK DOG OF DEPRESSION

"I'm afraid the black dog has really got me. Churchill's image of despair suits me better than 'the black hole.' A black hole just swallows you up. Would that it were that easy, to sink down into darkness, as if sleeping. But this dog, this dog! It crouches in the corner of the room, waits for me to make a move. Or lies at the foot of the bed, like a shadow, until I try to get up.

"Growls, and will not let me up.

"I go nowhere alone; he is at my side. He stands between me and any other, while I'm looking good, staying calm, smiling to disarm his ferocity....The dog stands in the way."[1]

This is the way Kathy Cronkite, author of *On the Edge of Darkness,* describes her depression. This disease has been described as a "broad-brush" term because it has many causes and means many different things to people who have experienced it.

What does depression mean to you? Everyone has been there to some degree. You may feel depressed because your parents are separating or because your favorite shirt got ruined. Your friend may feel depressed because she has to move or because her flight is canceled. Your computer crashes, the rain spoils an outdoor event, or the car won't start are just a few depressing things. You grieve after the loss of a loved one, you are sad after a relationship ends, and some days you just feel blue. Big things, little things, almost anything can make a person feel depressed, but the disease called depression is much more: it is feeling low, long term.

DEPRESSION IS MORE THAN A BAD DAY

If you are really depressed, you have more than a bad day or two. You feel worthless, sad, lonely, dumb, and unloved. You feel guilty and mistreated. Nothing matters anymore. You may experience depression without recognizing it, even when depression is so severe you feel you are locked up in a cage without a key. Although you may feel you are being drowned by a black wave, depression is a disease with a cure. It is a brain disorder in which there is an imbalance of chemicals in your brain. No matter how depressed you are, with help, you may feel good again.

Depression is a painful disease that is the most common form of mental illness and the number one cause of disability in the world today. The twenty-first century appears to be ushering in the Age of Melancholy as a follow-up to the Age of Anxiety, as the twentieth century was sometimes known. Your generation is at greater risk of depression than that of your parents, and they in turn were at greater risk than their parents. This increasing risk for each generation extends worldwide.[2]

Twenty-one-year-old Brandon kept his depression a secret. He thought it was a weakness, so he kept his feelings to himself. He buried his sadness in sports, training at every available moment. When he was mountain climbing, he had to focus on surviving. It was a wonderful way to stop thinking, to get rid of the pain of his depression. But he could not climb mountains all the time. Brandon felt that a "real man" would get over depression without help from anyone else. To him, there was something disgraceful about it.

Sixteen-year-old Marni hates to get out of bed in the morning because she wakes up tired, anxious, sad, and sometimes angry. She never wants to do things like play soccer or go to a rock concert. Her life seems hopeless, flat, and devoid of pleasure. Marni thinks she is not good enough to be anyone's friend. To her, the future looks grim, and there are days when she feels that life is not worth living. She thinks of suicide at least once a month, and her friends feel they should help her, but they ask, "Why is Marni depressed?" "What does she have to be depressed about?" Marni seems to have everything anyone can want. She is very bright, has artistic talent, two parents who love her, friends, and a new car that she got on her sixteenth birthday.

They feel like telling Marni, "Snap out of it" or "Pull yourself together," but willpower alone cannot help a person with depression to feel better any more than it can help someone with epilepsy to stop having epileptic seizures.[3]

DEPRESSION IS STILL A MYSTERY

Why is depression, one of the most common and most destructive illnesses in the United States today,[4] still something of a mystery? It may actually be many diseases, with different causes, different symptoms, and varying degrees of suffering. Depression is a condition of the mind, a physical affliction, an environmentally induced disease, one with a genetic tendency, and a biochemical illness. Depression has many features and dimensions. In spite of a great amount of research, it still mystifies people.

WHO IS DEPRESSED?

About 19 million adults in the United States suffer from depressive disorders today.[5] Depression affects more Americans than cancer, AIDS, or coronary heart disease. About one in five Americans will develop a mood disorder (usually depression) at some point in his or her life.[6] It may happen to you or a friend or a relative of any age. Many of the people who suffer from a depressive illness will be unnecessarily incapacitated for weeks or months because their illness goes unrecognized or untreated.[7]

You may know someone who is clinically depressed but doesn't seek treatment because he or she does not know it is a treatable illness. Perhaps this person doesn't know where to go for help or is ashamed. You may think of depression as an incurable disease that has a stigma attached to it, but depression appears to be a matter of brain chemistry. Many depressed people blame themselves or are blamed by their family and friends. The great majority of depressed people, however, can be helped.[8]

Did you ever wonder why people commit suicide? Why would someone like Kurt Cobain, who seemed to have it all, kill himself? Many drugs, like heroin and cocaine, can bring on depression and lead to suicide.

Kurt Cobain, a depressed rock star who killed himself

As many as 15 percent of those who suffer from some form of depression take their lives each year.[9] Some are convinced that suicide is the only cure for their suffering. Many of these people may have been too embarrassed to ask for help because they believed the myth that depressed people have a weak character.

DEPRESSION IN YOUNG CHILDREN

Ashley just celebrated her fifth birthday, but she was no more wild that day than usual. She shows excitability every day, has sleeping problems, often refuses to stop playing when it is mealtime, argues when her mother tells her to share, and generally misbehaves. Ashley may be suffering from depression; unable to express her true feelings, she acts out.

Until about the middle of the twentieth century, doctors did not believe that depression occurred in children and adolescents. Today, depression in the young is recognized as a disease, but the symptoms are often difficult to identify. A study sponsored by the National Institutes of Health estimated that more than 6 percent of children suffer from depression and 4.9 percent of them have major depression. The study also found that the onset of depression is occurring earlier in life currently than it did in the past.[10]

When children suffer from depression, they may, like Ashley, behave in ways that do not seem connected with being sad. They may express their problems through symptoms masked as truancy, disobedience, and self-destructive acts, as severe as suicide. After one young boy ran in the street in front of traffic several times, his parents took him to a therapist. Through play therapy, the therapist had the boy make up stories about dolls. As she watched him play, she was able to get ideas about how he felt. During one session, he made the mother doll throw the baby doll out the window, commenting that the child was bad and that the mother didn't really want him.

The therapist concluded that he probably considered himself bad and his life worthless. His risky behavior was a way of trying to harm himself because he was unlovable and unwanted. In contrast, some depressed children are so well behaved that they are often considered model children; parents and teachers do not realize that these children may be depressed underneath.

Since very young children cannot always explain their feelings in words, the only clues to their depression may be obtained through careful observation of their behavior.

TEENS AND DEPRESSION

Could you be depressed? More teens suffer from depression now than they did in the past. According to the National Depressive and Manic-Depressive Association, about one in ten teens will experience some form of depression.[11] A significant number of them are at risk for suicide.

Many teenagers who are depressed also have problems with alcohol or other drugs. They may use drugs to self-medicate in an effort to escape from depression. Sometimes the drug itself, or withdrawal from it, may cause the depression. Some adolescents use stimulants that increase aggressive

Caffeine, found in coffee, and cocaine are two types of stimulants people use to escape depression. However, in many cases, use of a stimulant only makes depression worse.

behavior, with tragic results that might have been avoided if they had received medical treatment for depression. It is not known whether depression precipitates acting out, whether predisposition for acting out leads to depression, or whether underlying causal factors are responsible for the joint display of such problems.[12]

The idea of self-mutilation seems strange to most people, but it is sometimes a way of expressing depression. Brianna had a history of depression after her stepfather sexually

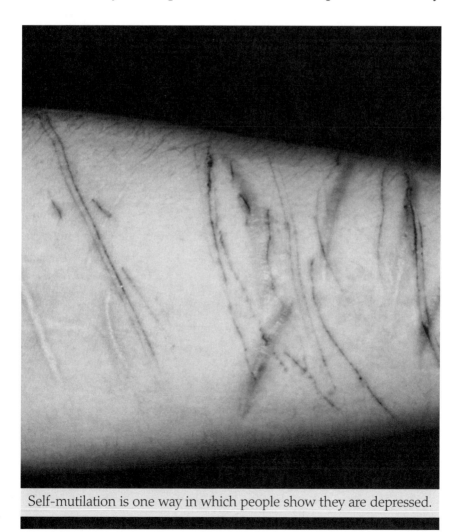

Self-mutilation is one way in which people show they are depressed.

abused her. One summer afternoon when she was home alone, she saw a scissors lying on a table nearby. She was feeling angry because friends did not include her in their trip to a rock concert, and the scissors just seemed to be there, inviting her to cut her arms aimlessly. She cried hysterically as she sliced her skin. Later she explained that by inflicting external pain on herself, she was trying to stop the dead feeling inside her. Some reports indicate that depression can be linked to an increased level of irritation and aggression.[13] No one knows how often tragic events are connected with depression.

OLDER PEOPLE

Depression can affect people of all ages, and it is common among the elderly. The brains of older people are more vulnerable to chemical abnormalities, their lives present many difficulties, and they are more likely than young people to be sedentary. Lack of exercise is a common contributor to depression. Thirty percent of people over 65 are expected to suffer from clinical depression over a period of three years.[14]

Memory problems in older people are not always due to senility or Alzheimer's disease. Depressed people may have lapses of memory and difficulty concentrating, and serious depression is sometimes mistaken for the beginning of Alzheimer's disease. While loss of memory and other mental problems of Alzheimer's disease are permanent and progressive, memory problems associated with depression are temporary and reversible with proper treatment.

DEPRESSION CAN BE A LIFE-THREATENING DISEASE

Have you ever noticed that you get a cold after you have been upset or have been feeling down? Depressed people get colds more frequently than other people.

Depressed people get colds more often than most people.

Even more dramatic is the finding that someone who is depressed is more likely to suffer from a heart attack than someone who is not depressed.[15] People who have heart attacks or heart surgery are at risk for depression. Studies are underway on the connection between heart disease and depression.[16] Among other reports, the National Institute of Mental Health has issued "Depression Can Break Your Heart."

Depression can be the cause of death in more direct ways, too. According to the National Institute of Mental Health, almost all people who kill themselves have a mental disorder, most commonly depression or a substance abuse disorder. Thirty-five percent of children who suffer from depression have had thoughts about wanting to die.[17]

While most people with depression do not commit suicide, depression increases the risk of suicide or suicide attempts. Some of the things you need to know about suicide are discussed later in this book.

NOTES

1. Kathy Cronkite, *On the Edge of Darkness: Conversations About Conquering Depression* (New York: Doubleday, 1994), Prologue. Used with permission.
2. Daniel Goleman, *Emotional Intelligence* (New York: Bantam Books, 1995), p. 240.
3. "Are Antidepressants Addictive?" *Health News* (February 2000): 10.
4. http://www.depression.org/biochem/html
5. http://www.nimh.nih.gov.publicat/depression.cfm
6. Simeon Margolis and Karen Swartz, *Depression and Anxiety* (Baltimore, MD: The Johns Hopkins Medical Institutions, 2000), p. 4
7. http://www.nimh.nih.gov/publicat/numbers.cfm
8. http://www.nimh.nih.gov/publict/depression/cfm
9. http://www.sciam.com/1998/0698issue/0698nemeroff/html
10. www.nimh.nih.gov/publicat/depchildresfact.cmf
11. http://www.ndmda.org/justmood.htm
12. http://www.nimh.nih.gov/publicat/violenceresfact.cfm
13. Ann Holmes, *Cutting Away the Pain: Understanding Self-Mutilation.* (Philadelphia: Chelsea House, 2000), p. 27.
14. Dharma Singh Khalsa, *Brain Longevity* (New York: Warner Books, 1997), p. 182.
15. http://www.nimh.nih.gov/publicat/heartbreak.cfm
16. Ibid.
17. http://www.1danat1.org/articles/seab/weinberg/

Chapter Two

WHY DEPRESSION?

Tanya is an attractive 15-year-old who leads a life without pleasure because she can't summon up much interest in anything or anybody. No one can really make friends with her because she does not seem to have any emotions. She says she feels dead inside. Tanya doesn't know what is wrong with her, but the doctor has told her she is suffering from depression. "Why am I depressed?" is a question she asks herself.

People who are clinically depressed cannot answer the question of why they feel the way they do. Possible causes of depression are almost as plentiful as the number of people who suffer from the disease. One thing is known, however: Depression is not caused by weakness of character, even though many people still think it is. A great many Americans still believe that depression is a form of laziness. They are ignorant of the fact that it is the most common mental illness.

AN ANCIENT AFFLICTION

Many teens have never heard of depression as a disease, but it has probably existed since prehistoric times. If you lived in one of the earliest civilizations in Egypt or the Near East, you would probably have believed that gods or evil spirits caused depression. The ancient Hebrews believed that mental illness was God's punishment for sin and that priests could cure it.

In the Bible, King Saul is said to be suffering a mental illness, needing David's music to soothe his melancholy.

If you had lived in early Greece or Rome, you would not have blamed outside forces such as spirits because you would probably have been exposed to more scientific methods of explaining abnormal behavior. The famous Greek physician Hippocrates, who lived in the fourth century B.C., was one of the first to apply rational thought to mental illness. His writings stated that sickness occurred when the body's four important "humors"—blood, yellow bile, black bile, and phlegm—were out of balance. Depression was attributed to an excess of black bile and was treated by various physical remedies such as bleeding, drugs, and diet.

Hippocrates

Aretaeus, a Roman physician who lived in the first century, was one of the first to describe mania and depression as manifestations of the same illness. The greatest Roman physician, Claudius Galen, who lived in the second century A.D. consolidated the ideas of the Greeks and wrote *On Melancholia*, a treatise that would influence theories about depression for hundreds of years. Then this enlightened age came to an end. During the Middle Ages, the theory of possession by demons or spirits was revived, and mentally ill people were now thought to be under the influence of the devil.

Through the years, people believed that all the mentally ill (then known as insane) were incurable. In the eighteenth century, many asylums were built throughout Europe; the first

Claudius Galen

mental asylum in the United States opened in 1773 in Williamsburg, Virginia. At that time, there was complete ignorance of the workings of the brain, and the strange symptoms of mental illness were regarded with dread. A depressed person who would not follow the rules of the asylum was often beaten. Some of these ill people were even starved and ridiculed.

Three centuries ago, if you were so depressed that you could not comply with instructions, you might be placed in a straitjacket attached to a wall. This and other punishments were administered in the belief that the more painful the treatment, the better the cure. Even King George III (the last English monarch to rule the American colonies) was treated in this manner for his mental disorder.

King George III was treated for being mentally ill.

In 1791, Philippe Pinel, a French psychiatrist and neurologist, played a major role in reforming the treatment of the mentally ill by introducing to mental hospitals a humane approach to the patients. He was one of a number of reformers who helped to change society's attitude toward the mentally ill. Benjamin Rush made similar reforms in the United States at about the same time. Until this period, patients with mental disorders were not considered to be sick or to be deserving of medical treatment; rather, they were thought to have some responsibility in causing their strange behavior. Unlike most of his contemporaries, Pinel believed that mental illness was caused mainly by heredity and by influences from the environment.

French psychiatrist Philippe Pinel (left, pointing), who strove to make treatments for mental illness more humane

Some depressed people who lived at the end of the nineteenth century, when Sigmund Freud (1856–1939) began to formulate his psychological theories and usher in the era of modern psychiatry, were more fortunate than their eighteenth-century forebears who were beaten and starved. Doctors started to listen to what patients had to say and to help many of them to feel better through what was called the talking cure. Freud's theories about the unconscious part of the mind revolutionized the practice of psychiatry. According to his theory, unconscious repressed feelings are the cause of psychological problems. By getting patients to talk freely and thus uncover conflict-causing unconscious feelings, therapists are able to help them understand and resolve their problems. Freud theorized that depression comes from anger turned against oneself.

Famous nineteenth-century psychiatrist Sigmund Freud

Using today's medical tools to scan the brain, scientists have learned more about its function and its biology. We now know that chemical imbalance in the brain plays a major role in depression and other mental illnesses. Today it is generally accepted that both environment and biology are involved in causing depression.

BLUE GENES

Has anyone in your family ever been depressed? If your mother or father or even a grandparent suffered from depression, you may carry some genes that make you more likely to be depressed at some time in your life. Many genes appear to be involved.[1]

Depression may afflict some families generation after generation. Does this happen simply because a person who grows up with a depressed parent tends to follow the same pattern? Studies reveal a 40 to 45 percent rate of psychiatric disorders among children of parents with mood disorders, and most of these disorders are depression.[2] Studies with adopted children and twins who were separated at birth seem to show that depression has a genetic influence.

Jacob, for example, was adopted when he was 6 weeks old from a hospital where his mother was confined for clinical depression. His adoptive parents, who were professional social workers, made every effort to help Jacob develop self-esteem and enjoy good physical and mental health. But despite their efforts, when Jacob was 12 years old, he showed signs of serious depression. He insisted that other kids did not like him. He hated himself and the way he looked, even though most people thought he was a handsome boy. Some mornings Jacob did not even want to get out of bed. His doctor diagnosed his problem as clinical depression. Even though he had never known his biological mother, he suffered from the same symptoms that she had.

Almost no one questions the theory that depression runs in families. In six studies of twins, depression was found to be present in 40 percent of identical twins but in only 17 percent of fraternal twins.[3] When a parent suffers from depression, a child is more likely to suffer from it than if neither parent suffered from this mood disorder. Children who receive an altered gene are predisposed, or more vulnerable, but they do not necessarily develop depression. Protective factors in the environment can play a part in preventing the expression of the "blue genes."

BRAIN CHEMISTRY

Scientists have discovered some of the things that go wrong when messages travel from one cell to the next in your brain, and they have also identified some of the chemicals that affect moods. When one considers the complex makeup of the brain, it is not surprising that some things can go wrong.

One hundred million nerve cells form the circuitry of the brain where communication takes place by way of electrical stimulation and chemical changes. Information travels across fibers called axons. These axons branch into smaller fibers and end in terminals. Electrical stimulation of a nerve cell causes the release of *neurotransmitters*, chemicals that carry messages between nerve cells. More than one hundred neurotransmitters have been identified.

What happens when tiny packets of neurotransmitters are released from the tip of a nerve cell? They cross a miniscule space known as a *synapse*. The synapse is about 20 millionths of a millimeter wide. The transfer happens at a speed that is inconceivable. In less than 1/5000 of a second, a neurotransmitter leaps the space to another nerve cell with its message. The receptor on the other nerve cell catches the message and is translated into action.

The chemistry of your brain is fragile, and it is special to you. That is, no one else's brain is exactly like yours. The causes of depression in your brain may be different from its causes in another person. Even the chemicals that are involved with changes in mood may be different, but in many cases a defect in the regulation of the release of one of three neurotransmitters may play a part.

THE SEROTONIN IN YOUR BRAIN

One of the neurotransmitters that plays a part in whether or not you are depressed is *serotonin*. There might not be enough serotonin for your brain's needs, or there might not be an adequate number of receptor sites to receive the serotonin. Perhaps not enough serotonin is produced, or serotonin may be taken back up and sucked into the cell that made it before it reaches the receptor sites. One of these problems, among others, can lead to inadequate supplies of the chemical and thus produce the symptoms of depression.

OTHER MOOD CHEMICALS

In addition to serotonin, other substances affect your moods, but not everyone's neurotransmitters are involved in the same way. *Norepinephrine* is one substance that plays a part in some cases but not in others. *Dopamine* is another neurotransmitter that may be involved, but evidence now suggests that dopamine, once implicated in depression, may play a more critical role in drug dependence than in mood disorders.[4] You may have heard of dopamine because of the part it plays in the brain's reward system. It is often mentioned in descriptions of how your body reacts to drugs.

The biology and chemistry of the causes of depression are complicated. Not even scientists completely understand them, but it is known that drugs that alter the expression of neurotransmitters produce mood changes.[5]

STRESS AND DEPRESSION

Stressful life events may play a large role in causing depression. Large amounts of a hormone known as *cortisol* are released into your bloodstream when your body is under stress, and many depressed people have high levels of it. This hormone is produced by the adrenal cortex glands located on top of your kidneys. Many depressed people don't have high levels of cortisol at the start of their disease,[6] but the increased amount of cortisol that comes with stress may perpetuate depression.[7]

Suppose you were in a serious accident when you were very young and one of your parents was killed. This stress could physically alter the way your brain functions in the future. The loss of one's parents, childhood abuse, car accidents, isolation, serious illness or death in the immediate family, extreme sibling rivalry, or other childhood traumas can increase the chances of depression later in life.

EMOTIONAL LOSS

Many studies have suggested that a definite relationship exists between emotional loss in the young and the development of depression. What do you think would happen to you if scientists put you in a cage with no other people, no computer games, no books, or anything that you could play or work with? Experiments with monkeys have shown that when infant monkeys were separated from their mothers and were deprived of any stimulation for several weeks, they became apathetic and appeared depressed. When they were placed with other monkeys, they did not play but instead remained huddled in a corner. Other experiments with monkeys have shown that even short periods of separation from the mother have long-term effects such as arrested social development.

Human babies separated from their mothers react in a similar fashion. A kind of depression called hospitalism used to be seen in institutions where children did not receive enough mothering. These children became apathetic and withdrawn, even though they were well cared for physically. Today volunteers in many hospital settings cuddle babies to prevent this condition.

In some countries, abandoned babies are raised in orphanages and receive no attention other than feeding, clothing changes, and occasional bathing. Doctors warn people who want to adopt these babies that lack of caring in infancy or other deprivation may make a person more sensitized to loss and susceptible to depression later in life. The loss may be physical or emotional, and the emotional loss may range from outright emotional abuse to subtle and hidden hostility.

GENDER

Women around the world are twice as likely to suffer from depression as men.[8] Sex hormones seem to be the logical reason for this disparity, but other factors may also be involved. Menstruation and pregnancy do not usually lead to depression. However, depression may be triggered in women if they are unable to have children, if they suffer miscarriages, or if they undergo surgical menopause. Many women are particularly vulnerable after the birth of a baby, suffering from a disorder known as *postpartum depression*, a condition described later in this book.

Consider Tish, a single mother who generally felt out of control and helpless. She worked a full day, picked up her children at day care, tried to spend quality time with them, ran errands, cleaned the house, prepared dinner, and cared for the pets. Not having enough time in the day to complete all the necessary tasks, she felt she was a failure. She was also subject to the whims of everyone, from her babies to her boss. She became seriously depressed and spent much of her time in bed before her family insisted she see a doctor. After Tish began a program of medication and sought therapy for her depression, she was able to take control of her life.

While hormonal changes may be partly responsible for women being more vulnerable to depression than men are, recent research has emphasized other contributing factors, such as the lack of mastery in women's lives, the stress of too much responsibility, and the tendency of women to talk about their problems rather than take action. Psychologists emphasize the importance of taking control of one's life as the solution for depression.[9]

Prevalence of Depression				
Age	Males	% of age group with depression	Females	% of age group with depression
12–17 years	41,050	—	93,423	8.3
18–24 years	79,408	6.6	127,695	10.8
25–44 years	156,139	3.5	404,229	8.6
45–64 years	94,546	3.5	183,333	6.3
65 +	22,309	—	53,475	3.1

— amount too small to be expressed

Source: Statistics Canada, National Population Health Survey, 1995

This chart illustrates the difference in the rate of depression between men and women.

LEARNED HELPLESSNESS

Do you have a friend who is always negative about what he or she can do? According to cognitive theory, depressed people exhibit an erroneous way of thinking. They feel that what happens to them is not under their control, and so no matter what they do, nothing will turn out right. They feel inadequate and unworthy, they experience the world as a hostile, demanding place, and they expect failure and punishment in their future.

Selig's family, which was very critical of him, taught him to see everything in a negative way. He perceived every setback as proof that he was completely inadequate and worthless, and he felt hopeless about his future. He was passive and resigned himself to accepting painful situations as inevitable and to enduring his feelings of being overwhelmed and helpless. The condition of learned helplessness has been produced in dogs experimentally. In people, learned helplessness can be unlearned. When Selig learned that he could be the master of his own life and was able to take some positive action to change things, his depression began to lift.

DEPRESSION'S TRAVELING COMPANIONS

Changes in the neurotransmitters of depressed people's brains put them at risk for some physical diseases. As mentioned earlier, depression and heart disease are common companions, with one often leading to the other.

Many different physical conditions can be mistaken for depression or can be involved in causing it. Thyroid disease, Parkinson's disease, stroke, cancer, and other medical illnesses can cause depression. Research studies have also linked depression with diabetes, obesity, AIDS, and other major illnesses.

Suppose you suffer from depression and have found that drinking can make you feel better. You might drink so much and so often, however, that you become addicted to alcohol. It is not uncommon for young people suffering from depression to self-medicate and to get relief by drinking. Here too, the arrows can go in both directions. Many depressed teens drink and become alcoholics, and many alcoholics become depressed.

Abuse of drugs other than alcohol can put people at risk for depression and substance abuse often coexists with depression. About one-third of people with depression also have a substance abuse problem.[10] Some prescription drugs also cause depression. If you are taking a prescription drug, you should ask your doctor if it can cause depression.

Seventeen-year-old Nancy suffers from panic disorder—disabling attacks of terrible anxiety that strike unexpectedly. During these attacks, Nancy's heart races, she sweats, she becomes dizzy, and she feels as though she is going to die or go crazy. This disorder occurs mostly in young adults, between late adolescence and their mid-thirties. Many of those afflicted also suffer from depression.

Serious eating disorders such as anorexia nervosa and bulimia seem to be on the rise among teenage girls and young women. Recent studies show that 15 percent of young women have unhealthy attitudes and behaviors about food; many girls begin to worry about their weight and go on diets as early as age 8 or 9. Between 50 and 75 percent of those with eating disorders have a lifetime history of depression.[11]

DEPRESSION IS NOT INFECTIOUS

Depression is frequently caused by a combination of genetic, psychological, and environmental factors. The causes are many and varied, and not everything is known about why people develop depression. One thing seems certain, however: You will not catch depression from helping someone who suffers from it.

NOTES

1. http://www.nimh.nih.gov/publicat/invisible.cfm

2. Mark S. Gold, *The Good News About Depression* (New York: Random House, 1997), p. 287.

3. Ibid., p. 198.

4. Simeon Margolis and Karen L. Swartz, *Depression and Anxiety* (Baltimore, MD: Johns Hopkins White Papers, 2000), p. 9.

5. Samuel H. Barondes, *Molecules and Mental Illness* (New York: Scientific American Library, 1999), p. 132.

6. "Why Depression Still Mystifies Us," An Interview with Dr. Raymond DePaulo, Jr., *Cerebrum, The Dana Forum of Brain Science* (New York: Dana Press, Winter 2000), p. 51.

7. Ibid, p. 136.

8. Robert E. Hales and Dianne Hales, *The Mind/Mood Pill Book* (New York: Bantam Books, 2000), p. 321

9. wysiwyg://23/http://www.intelihealth.com/IH/ihtIH/EMIHC000/333/333/274775.html

10. http:www.nimh.nih.gov/publicat/abuse.cfm

11. http://www.nimh.nih.gov/publicat/abuse.cfm

Chapter Three

DEPRESSION HAS MANY FACES

CAN YOU RECOGNIZE DEPRESSION?

Have you ever expressed the following sentiments: "No one will ever love me, I will live and die alone. I will go nowhere fast. I will be nothing at all. The promise that a beautiful life lies on the other side of depression, a life worth surviving suicide for, will have turned out to be false. It will all have been a big dupe."[1] A depressed person may feel this way much of the time.

It's normal to feel sad or down now and then. But if you are feeling blue most of the time and are having trouble in school or in your relationships with family and friends, your problem may be clinical depression. Clinical depression is not just a temporary blue mood. It is a serious medical condition—a whole-body illness that affects your mood, thoughts, behavior, and health. Depression interferes with every part of your life, and it needs to be treated.

A dozen types of depression have been identified.[2] There are three main types: *major depressive disorder (unipolar major depression)*, in which a sad mood predominates; *manic-depressive disorder (bipolar disorder)*, in which sad moods alternate with episodes of feeling high; and *dysthymic disorder (dysthymia)*, which is less severe than major depressive disorder, but is a more chronic form of depression. Dysthymia is discussed in the next chapter.

MAJOR DEPRESSIVE DISORDER (UNIPOLAR)

Major depression always causes some degree of emotional distress or interferes with a person's ability to function. The symptoms affect all areas of everyday life, including people's family relationships and friendships, their ability to work or go to school, and their ability to eat, sleep, and engage in pleasurable activities. Episodes of depression may occur several times in a person's life, and in some cases no obvious cause can be found. A stressful event, a major disappointment in one's life, or the loss of a loved one can sometimes trigger a serious depression. The normal grieving process that takes place after someone dies is not the same as major depression, even though the bereaved person feels depressed. A diagnosis of major depression is made only if the symptoms last more than two months after the loss, or if the person has marked difficulty in functioning, experiences severe slowing of thoughts, or is preoccupied with strong feelings of worthlessness.

Some depressed people may deny feeling sad, but facial expression and body language often betray the sadness within. Many depressed people act as though they are generally slowed down in their movements, speech, and thinking. They speak very slowly, revealing little expression in their voices and pausing for a long time before answering questions. Often, they seem subdued and speak less than usual; some severely depressed individuals refuse to speak at all.

Instead of becoming slowed down, other depressed people may become agitated. Unable to sit still, they pace about nervously, wringing their hands or pulling on their clothing or hair. They may feel anxious all the time or worry excessively about their physical health.

Depressed people may have recurring thoughts about their own death. These thoughts may range from a belief that it would be better if they were dead to momentary, occasional thoughts of committing suicide, to the actual planning of suicide. People with serious intentions of committing suicide may obtain a gun or other means of killing themselves and may have specific plans about when and where they are going to do it. Anyone who talks about suicide should be taken seriously because no one can accurately predict whether a certain individual will commit suicide. Even someone who has only fleeting thoughts about suicide may be at high risk, depending on the circumstances.

Describing the symptoms of depression varies from one culture to another. Complaints of "nerves" in Latino cultures, "imbalance" in Asian culture, or "heartbreak" among the Hopi are examples of the differing ways in which people describe their experience of depression.[3]

DEPRESSION CAN BE VERY DIFFERENT

Consider the following stories that are based on actual cases. The individuals are all different, but they have something in common: They all suffer from major depression.

Theo was a straight-A student in high school until the end of his junior year, when his grades began slipping. He couldn't concentrate enough to finish his homework, and he lost interest in everything. He didn't even enjoy his favorite activity, playing hockey on the school team. He felt exhausted all the time, but he couldn't sleep. He began to drink a lot, but alcohol didn't help. Food didn't appeal to him, so he often skipped meals; having lost so much weight, he looked gaunt and unhealthy. His friends said he looked like a zombie and urged him to pull himself together, but he couldn't, and that made him feel even worse. He and his friends didn't realize that depression can strike people of all ages, including children and adolescents. Theo was one of the 4 out of 100 teenagers who get seriously depressed each year.[4]

Sixteen-year-old Jed's experience of depression was a little different. He became depressed after his parents told him they were getting a divorce. Although his parents assured him that he was not the cause, he blamed himself for breaking up their marriage. He was obsessed by feelings of guilt and worthlessness. Then he began to believe that he was the cause of other unfortunate occurrences. When his friend Roger wasn't chosen for the hockey team, for example, Jed was certain that it was his fault, and no one could convince him he was wrong. When he started hearing voices telling him he was bad, he decided that the best solution was suicide. He even began to plan ways of killing himself. He gave his best friend a few of his most treasured possessions because soon he wouldn't need them. Fortunately, Jed got help before it was too late.

Jed's case was extreme; his depression was so severe that it affected his thinking. He had *delusions*—false, fixed beliefs that had no basis in reality, and he experienced *auditory hallucinations*—he heard voices that other people did not hear.

In contrast to Theo and Jed, Kim didn't seem sad. At first no one knew what was wrong with her because she had changed from an easygoing 12-year-old into a perpetually cranky and irritable person. She picked fights with everybody, and she was so touchy that her friends now avoided her. Her parents simply thought she was going through a rebellious phase. Kim was not just acting in an obnoxious fashion; underneath she was depressed.

Mrs. Ortiz visited her family physician with complaints of nervousness and frequent headaches and pains in her stomach. The doctor found no medical illness, but when she and Mrs. Ortiz spent some time talking, it became clear that the problem was depression.

When Laura's Grandmother Rose lost her house keys a few times, misplaced some important papers somewhere in her house, and began having trouble concentrating, her family feared that she had *Alzheimer's disease*. This condition is a progressive, irreversible brain disease that strikes some older people, and one of its early signs is memory loss. In Grandmother Rose's case, depression caused her forgetfulness and her difficulty in concentrating; after she received treatment, she no longer had problems with her memory.

Farah's uncle had been treated for mild depression several times in the past, and he had always been able to carry on with his work while he was being treated. This time, however, he felt so tired that it was a tremendous effort even to wash, shave, and dress himself, and everything he did seemed to take twice as long as usual. He finally stopped getting dressed in the morning, and he spent most of the day in bed, just lying there staring at the ceiling, refusing to talk to anyone.

While most people lose their appetite when they get depressed, Sally went on an eating binge and gained thirty pounds. She hated being fat, but the emptiness inside seemed to lessen and she felt better when she filled herself with her favorite foods.

Charlie was a happy, bright, alert baby until his mother died suddenly when he was about a year old. After his mother's death, he was cared for by a succession of housekeepers, none of whom stayed more than a couple of months. Charlie became lethargic, withdrawn, and sad; he no longer smiled, and he stopped talking. By the time he was 2 years old, he looked like a mentally handicapped child.

COMMON SYMPTOMS

How can you tell the difference between a passing blue mood and clinical depression? If you or someone you know has five or more of the symptoms listed below, and if these symptoms are present every day and persist for more than two weeks, it's a sign of serious depression.

SYMPTOMS OF MAJOR DEPRESSION

You feel sad or cry a lot, and those feelings won't go away, or you seem to have no feelings.

You've lost interest or pleasure in activities that you used to enjoy, like sports, or going out with friends.

You are tired all the time and feel slowed down, or you feel agitated and restless, and you can't sit still.

You feel hopeless, life seems meaningless, and you think nothing will ever change. You feel worthless, you think you aren't any good to anyone, and you feel guilty without reason, or you seem to be numb and have no feelings at all.

You have trouble falling asleep, you wake up much earlier than usual, or you oversleep.

You don't have an appetite and you've lost weight, or you are eating more than usual.

You can't concentrate or make up your mind, and you have trouble remembering things.

You are irritable, and you lose your temper over little things.

You have headaches, stomachaches, or other aches and pains that are not explained by another condition.

You think about death or suicide.

SYMPTOMS IN CHILDREN AND TEENS

Children and teenagers do not always express feelings of sadness or show the same symptoms that adults do, but even infants and very young children can suffer from depression when they are neglected, as in Charlie's case. As mentioned earlier, mental health experts did not believe that children could suffer from depression until about the middle of the twentieth century. Before that time the symptoms were considered a behavioral disorder, or were ignored. Depression went unrecognized for so long in part because many depressed children are well-behaved, shy, and very quiet; they don't cause any trouble at home or in school. The kids who get noticed are the mischievous ones, those with behavioral disorders. No one notices that some of the quiet children are depressed; they may not look as sad or slowed down as depressed adults, but they are suffering nonetheless.

Depressed children tend to keep to themselves and not interact with others.

SYMPTOMS OF DEPRESSION IN CHILDREN

The following are warning signs that may mean a child is depressed:

Skipping school frequently or falling behind in schoolwork

Running away from home or talking about running away

Temper outbursts and unexplained anger, or frequent complaints

Frequent physical complaints, for example, stomachaches or headaches

Feeling bored all the time

Shy behavior such as keeping away from other people and not communicating

Extreme sensitivity to rejection or failure; disappointment when things don't go as planned

Low self-esteem

Difficulty in relationships with friends or family

Fear of death

Reckless behavior

Researchers at the National Institute of Mental Health (NIMH) estimate that about 5 percent of 9- to 17-year-olds suffer from major depression.[5] Depression in children and adolescents presents a special challenge for mental health professionals for several reasons. Some health professionals are reluctant to label a young person with a diagnosis of mental illness because of the stigma attached to this diagnosis. Major depression often goes unrecognized in young people because the signs are frequently brushed aside as normal mood swings that are typical of a particular age group. The main symptoms of depression are the same in children and adolescents as they are in adults. But symptoms may vary depending on the individual's stage of development; moreover the dividing line between normal and abnormal is less distinct in children. Behavior that is normal in young children, such as temper tantrums or fearfulness, may be a sign of mental illness at another age. Children and younger adolescents often are unable to pinpoint exactly how they feel, and they may not have the vocabulary to describe their inner feelings. Depressed children may act out their sad feelings through their behavior instead of through words. This makes it more difficult for parents, teachers, and health care workers to decipher the problem.

Josh was a happy 6-year-old until his father's work took him away from home for several months. Soon after his father left, Josh began to lose interest in schoolwork and frequently disrupted the class. At home he was demanding and clingy, and he suddenly developed a fear of the dark. Josh didn't know how to explain what he felt, but after his mother, the teacher, and the school psychologist had a conference, they realized that Josh was depressed. His father's absence had probably triggered the depression. He was not just being disobedient or "going through a phase."

It is very important to find out what is wrong and to get treatment as soon as possible because most people with depression, even those who are seriously ill, can be helped—and the earlier they seek help, the better. It is especially urgent for children and adolescents with depression because they have an increased risk of repeated episodes that continue into adulthood. They also have an increased risk of psychological problems even after the depression has lifted. In addition, young people with prolonged illness suffer delays in their development; the normal process of growing up is interrupted. They may fall behind in school and lose contact with their friends. Adolescents with depression have an increased risk of substance abuse and suicide. Among seriously depressed children and adolescents, as many as 7 percent may commit suicide in their young adult years.[6] Knowing how to recognize depression and getting help for it may save a life.

MANIC-DEPRESSIVE ILLNESS (BIPOLAR DISORDER)

Manic-depressive illness, or bipolar disorder, is a serious mental illness involving episodes of major depression that alternate episodes of mania (periods of greatly increased energy and elated feelings that are sometimes uncontrollable) with periods of normal mood. In some cases, the symptoms of depression and mania are present together at the same time. The person experiences severe swings in mood, cycling from elation to the deepest despair. Manic-depressive illness is extremely distressing and disruptive for the 2 million people who are afflicted. It also makes life difficult for the people around them—families, friends, teachers, and employers—who must cope with outrageous and sometimes dangerous behavior. Like major depression, it tends to run in families.

SIGNS OF A MANIC EPISODE

Here are the signs of a manic episode:[7]

A period of excessively elated feelings or extreme irritability

Increased energy and activity or restlessness

Racing thoughts, constantly jumping from one subject to the next

Rapid, nonstop talking

Distractibility

Decreased need for sleep

Unrealistic beliefs in one's abilities and powers; overly inflated self-esteem

Poor judgment that is out of character: risky behavior, such as buying sprees; foolish business ventures; or inappropriate sexual advances

MANIC EPISODES

A diagnosis of manic episode is made if the abnormally elevated mood lasts a week or more, if the person shows three or more of the other symptoms listed, if the person's ability to function at work or in social relationships becomes seriously impaired, or if hospitalization is needed to prevent them from harming themselves and others.

The mood states in bipolar disorder can be thought of as a continuous range, with severe depression at one end, shading into moderate depression, mild depression or the blues, to normal mood, then a mild form of mania known as *hypomania,* and at the far end, mania. Some people with bipolar disorder have repeated bouts of depression and only an occasional episode of hypomania. Others experience repeated episodes of mania but only infrequent episodes of depression.

In her book *An Unquiet Mind,* Dr. Kay Redfield Jamison describes her lifelong struggle with manic-depressive illness. Her first attack came when she was a senior in high school. She recounts racing around "like a crazed weasel," immersed in sports, bubbling with plans, staying up all night, reading everything she found, writing poetry, believing that she understood complicated mathematical theories, and making completely unrealistic plans for the future. The world seemed perfect, and she felt really great; she could do anything. Her friends didn't share her enthusiasm and kept telling her to slow down.

She finally did slow down, but then she slid into depression. She found that she couldn't understand anything she read, and she couldn't follow what was presented in her classes. Nothing was interesting or enjoyable, and she wanted to die. Later she wrote that she was amazed that she survived those awful months on her own. These episodes were only the beginning of a long series of manic and depressive cycles that became worse.

During one of her later manic episodes, Dr. Jamison went on a shopping spree and bought twelve snakebite kits, expensive jewelry, three watches, furniture that she didn't need, and some totally inappropriate clothes. She thinks she may have shoplifted a blouse because she couldn't bear waiting on line for another minute. Some depressed people buy gifts for all their friends or give things to total strangers. Others may sell all their assets and risk financial ruin. One woman decided that she was tired of washing dishes for her family, so she stored her china and silverware in boxes, and bought enough paper plates and plastic utensils to last for years.

Even though Dr. Jamison was a scientist and professor of psychiatry, it took her a long time to admit that she had manic-depressive illness and that she needed medication. It is not unusual for people with manic-depressive disorder to resist taking medication and to deny that anything is wrong with them because the hypomanic state feels so good to them. They are very cheerful; they make jokes and clever puns or plays on words, and their humor is infectious; others laugh with them, not at them. A hypomanic episode is not severe enough to cause confusion or *psychosis* (inability to recognize reality), or to interfere seriously with a person's ability to function. Some creative and artistic people with manic-depressive illness have produced their best work while in a hypomanic state.

Manic-depressive illness left untreated tends to get worse. Hypomania may escalate to mania, and the feelings of euphoria and omnipotence may change to confusion, irritability, anger, and fear. People in the throes of full-fledged mania may become psychotic (i.e., lose touch with reality): they may hear voices or experience visions, and they may have delusional ideas. Often, the delusions involve grandiose beliefs about their powers. For example, a man may try to jump out a window because he thinks he can fly. Uncontrolled mania can lead to tragic consequences, including destruction of relationships with family and friends, loss of employment, financial disaster, and suicide.

In its early stages, bipolar disorder can be mistaken for other conditions. For example, some stimulants, such as cocaine or steroids, can cause manic-like states. Brain tumors and other medical conditions may cause mood changes.

MANIC DEPRESSION IN CHILDREN AND TEENS

Manic-depressive illness was previously considered rare in children under age 12, but findings from a recent study suggest that the illness may be as common in children and adolescents as it is in adults.[8] It is often difficult to recognize in children because the symptoms may not be exactly the same as in adults, and may be mistaken for normal mood changes and emotions. It may mimic *attention deficit/hyperactivity disorder (ADHD)* or other mental disorders that commonly occur in this age group.

Children and adolescents with mania are more likely to be irritable or prone to aggressive outbursts. This is in contrast to adults, who typically feel elated or high. Researchers think that bipolar disorder that begins in childhood or the early teens may be a different, more severe form of the illness. If a child or teenager appears depressed and exhibits symptoms of ADHD, disruptive behavior, excessive outbursts of temper, and mood changes, these are signals that may indicate bipolar disorder.

A study of adolescents between the ages of 14 and 18 revealed that teens with bipolar disorder had higher rates of anxiety and behavior disorders, suicide attempts, and use of mental health services compared to teens with major depression and those who had never been mentally ill. The study emphasized the need for better recognition, prevention, and treatment of bipolar disorder in adolescents.[9] Many pediatricians receive little training in psychiatry. One study at Duke University found that a group of pediatricians was able to identify only 17 percent of the children with psychiatric disorders.[10] Even psychiatrists and psychologists may not recognize bipolar disorder in children, so finding a knowledgeable expert is important. Misdiagnosis can have serious adverse effects. For example, stimulant medications are used to treat ADHD, but using stimulants in a child who actually has bipolar disorder may make the symptoms worse. Using medication that targets major depression in someone who has bipolar disorder can trigger a manic episode. Fortunately, most people with manic-depressive illness can be helped. Treating this disorder is discussed in Chapter 5.

NOTES

1. Elizabeth Wurtzel, *Prozac Nation: Young and Depressed in America* (New York: Riverhead Books, 1995), p. 3.
2. William S. Appleton, *Prozac and the New Antidepressants* (New York: Plume Books, Penguin Putnam, 2000), p. 31.
3. American Psychiatric Association, *Diagnostic and Statistical Manual of Mental Disorders,* 4th ed. (Washington, DC: American Psychiatric Association, 1994), p. 324.
4. Let's Talk About Depression, National Institute of Mental Health, www.nimh.nih.gov/depression/genpop/letstalk.htm
5. Depression in Children and Adolescents: A Fact Sheet for Physicians, National Institute of Mental Health, www.nimh.nih.gov/publicat/depchildresfact.cfm
6. Ibid.
7. American Psychiatric Association. *Diagnostic and Statistical Manual of Mental Disorders,* p. 332.
8. Child and Adolescent Bipolar Disorder: An Update from the National Institute of Mental Health, www.nimh.nih.gov/publicat/bipolarupdate.cfm
9. Ibid.
10. Mitzi Waltz, *Bipolar Disorders: A Guide to Helping Children and Adolescents* (Sebastopol, CA: O'Reilly and Associates, 2000), p. 31.

Chapter Four

OTHER KINDS OF DEPRESSION

Maura always enjoyed her summer vacations; she loved swimming and sunning herself at the beach. In the fall, while the weather was still pleasant, she liked to hike in the mountains. As winter approached, the hours of daylight decreased, and sometimes it was cloudy or rainy day after day. Every year at that season, she began feeling blue, and she didn't know why. Maura was suffering from a mild kind of depression known as SAD—seasonal affective disorder. Although most depression involves feelings of sadness, not all depressions are the same. SAD is one of several types of depression that are different from those discussed in Chapter 3.

SEASONAL AFFECTIVE DISORDER (SAD)

Some people who are normal and happy during most of the year become depressed every winter. They start feeling blue when the days get shorter in the fall, and they begin to feel better only as the hours of daylight increase in the spring. Some individuals experience episodes of depression at other times of the year, but this is less common except in people who live in places that have little sunshine. The prevalence of wintertime SAD is higher in more northern latitudes. For example, about 10 percent of people living in New Hampshire have SAD compared to fewer than 2 percent in Florida.[1]

If you have SAD, you probably feel tired and lethargic during the winter, and you tend to sleep more than usual.

Your appetite increases, you may have a craving for carbohydrates, and you may gain weight. When spring arrives, your energy returns, you lose weight, and your mood lifts.

No one knows exactly what causes SAD, but it may be related to a disruption of the internal clock that governs the *circadian* (24-hour) biological rhythms. This disruption may affect the production of the sleep-promoting hormone *melatonin.*

Sitting under special bright lights for a prescribed length of time every day seems to help most people with wintertime SAD. Morning light seems to be more effective in relieving symptoms than evening light, according to some studies.[2] The light may counteract the symptoms by resetting the person's biological clock. Taking winter vacations in a sunny climate is also an effective treatment. In some schools in Siberia, where days are short, children are routinely exposed to bright lights to prevent depression and to activate vitamin D. If symptoms of depression are severe and do not respond to light therapy, antidepressant medication may help.

DYSTHYMIC DISORDER (DYSTHYMIA)

Dysthymic disorder is a milder form of depression than major depression, but it lasts longer. A diagnosis of this disorder is made when a depressed mood is present almost every day for at least two years, or one year in the case of children and adolescents. It may last for many years and may even persist throughout a person's entire life. People who suffer from dysthymic disorder may describe themselves as being "down in the dumps" or gloomy all the time, and they often say they have always felt that way. They don't seem able to feel really happy or excited about anything, and they tend to worry a lot and suffer unnecessary guilt. Children and teens may be more irritable than sad.

SYMPTOMS OF DYSTHYMIA

In addition to feelings of sadness, two or more of the following additional symptoms are present in dysthymia:

Loss of appetite or overeating

Sleep problems

Lack of energy

Low self-esteem

Poor concentration

Feelings of hopelessness

Dysthymic disorder often begins early in life, and its onset is often insidious. As many as half of the people with this disorder go on to experience major depression or bipolar depression. People with both dysthymia and major depression are sometimes said to be suffering from double depression. As is the case for major depression, women are twice as likely as men to develop dysthymia. Researchers who studied twins have noted that if one of a pair of identical twins develops dysthymia, the other one often does as well.[3] Individuals with dysthymia frequently have other disorders such as anxiety, phobias, or substance abuse. In children, it may be associated with attention deficit/hyperactivity disorder, learning disorders, or conduct disorder.

Some mental health experts have noted that it is sometimes difficult to distinguish dysthymia from a depressive personality disorder, which is marked by a pattern of depressive thinking and behavior. Chronically gloomy mood, feelings of inadequacy or worthlessness, overly negative and critical attitude toward oneself and others, tendency to worry or feel guilty, and pessimistic outlook on life are traits that characterize these individuals. However, there are differences between the two conditions. People with depressive personality disorder are not necessarily sad; their disturbance involves the ways in which they view themselves and others. People with dysthymia have more symptoms of depression and experience more distress. A personality disorder is a pattern of thinking and relating to others that is evident early in life and does not change significantly, but dysthymia may develop at any age and may last only two years or less. The results of a study of young children in New Zealand suggest that a depressive temperament may in some cases develop into a mood disorder later in life. Depressive personality is common in the families of people with mood disorders.[4]

PSYCHOTIC DEPRESSION

About 15 percent of people with major depression, like 16-year-old Jed in Chapter 4, have delusions or hallucinations in addition to the usual symptoms of depression. These delusions or false beliefs usually involve guilt (feeling responsible for a loved one's illness or death), punishment (believing he or she deserves punishment for a sin or some personal failure), destruction (believing that the world will be destroyed), or bodily delusions (thinking that one's body is rotting). Common hallucinations consist of voices berating the person for being unworthy or bad. People with psychotic depression usually need to be hospitalized because their thinking and judgment are impaired, and they may put themselves and others at risk by acting on their mistaken beliefs. For example, someone who hears a voice telling him to kill himself as punishment for his sins is at great risk for suicide.

POSTPARTUM DEPRESSION

Perhaps you know a woman who got depressed after she had a baby. Depression may seem like a strange reaction because most women are excited and happy about a healthy new baby. This kind of depression is called post-partum depression (postpartum means after birth), and it begins within four weeks after a woman has given birth to a baby. The symptoms are the same as those of major depression. Many women experience a mild form of depression (called "baby blues") after the birth of a baby, but this is temporary and normal. Postpartum depression is more common in women who have had previous episodes of depression and is more severe and prolonged than baby blues. It strikes about 10 percent of new mothers, who may also experience anxiety, suicidal ideas, and frequently, serious thoughts about harming their babies. Many feel guilty about being depressed at a time when they should feel happy about a new baby. Some women—one or two of every thousand new mothers—become psychotic and may experience delusions and hallucinations involving their infants. A psychotic mother may believe that her baby is possessed by the devil. She may hear voices telling her to kill the baby. Women who commit infanticide are likely to be suffering from psychotic postpartum depression. A tragic example of this was Andrea Yates' bathtub drowning of her five small children in June 2001 in her home in Texas.

ATYPICAL DEPRESSION

People with atypical depression exhibit some features that characterize the typical major depression, such as loss of sense of pleasure, hopelessness, worthlessness, and guilt, but they have other features that differ from the usual symptoms of depression. A key feature of atypical depression is so-called *mood reactivity.* It means that the depressed individual is capable of being cheered up when something positive happens, such as receiving a compliment. In contrast, someone with typical depression is not likely to cheer up in response to a positive event or word. Other features that differ from typical major depression include increased appetite or weight gain instead of loss of appetite and increased need for sleep instead of insomnia. Instead of feeling worse in the morning, some people with atypical depression feel worse in the evening. This type of depression usually begins at an earlier age, often during high school. It affects two to three times as many females as males and tends to be more chronic, without complete recovery in between episodes.

Some kinds of depression are far more serious than others. A doctor can determine which kind is causing the symptoms and can help to treat the disease.

NOTES

1. American Medical Association, *Essential Guide to Depression* (New York: Pocket Books, 1998), p. 41.
2. "Three on SAD," *The Harvard Mental Health Letter* 15, no. 12 (June 1999): 6.
3. American Medical Association, *Essential Guide to Depression*, p. 39.
4. Daniel N. Klein, "Depressive Personality," *The Harvard Mental Health Letter* 16, no. 3 (September 1999): 4–6.

Chapter Five

DUMPING DEPRESSION THROUGH TREATMENT

TEEN COMMITS SUICIDE AFTER LONG PERIOD OF DEPRESSION

Edward Bland moved to his new apartment on Wednesday and killed himself the next day. He left a note saying that he was thinking of suicide for a long time but did not want to make a mess at home. Edward was 17 years old and had been diagnosed two years ago as having severe depression. His family did not approve of medication.

DO SOMETHING ABOUT DEPRESSION

If depression is not treated, it can get worse. It can last longer and it prevents you from enjoying life. Too often, untreated depression leads to suicide, but the symptoms of serious depression are not always recognized as danger signals. Depression has been called one of the most treatable illnesses. If you are depressed, you have an 80 percent chance of being helped. Sadly, nearly two out of three depressed people do not seek treatment[1] for a variety of reasons.

You may be tempted to tell someone who is depressed to snap out of it because there seems no reason to be so down. This is not the right approach to take. Since depression is a life-threatening disease, it is important to do something about it.

The first step to getting the right treatment for depression is a complete medical examination by your family physician. Certain medications as well as some medical conditions can cause the same symptoms as depression, so these causes must be ruled out by physical examination and laboratory tests. If a physical cause is ruled out, your doctor may refer you to a psychiatrist for evaluation.

The choice of treatment varies with the kind and severity of the depression. If you are mildly depressed, psychotherapy alone may help. But people with moderate to severe depression usually need *antidepressants,* and most do best with both medication and psychotherapy.

FINDING THE RIGHT MEDICATION

Antidepressants act to restore a person's normal mood. They are not "uppers" or stimulants, and they do not give you an artificial high. These drugs are not habit-forming, but they are powerful and should be taken only when prescribed by a doctor. In addition, the prescribed dosage should be followed exactly, and the drug should not be discontinued without a doctor's supervision. Alcohol and some medications—both prescription and over-the-counter drugs—can cause serious reactions when mixed with antidepressants. Some teens sell their drugs to others, even though they do not produce a high. There are over twenty different antidepressants on the market in the United States. The choice of drug depends on the person's symptoms, but it is not always possible to predict which one is best for any individual.

Antidepressants do not work immediately but usually take between one and three weeks before any improvement is seen. However, side effects may appear sooner. Patients and doctors must work together for a period of weeks to check for side effects, to monitor blood levels of the drug, and to see if the drug is helpful. Sometimes the dosage needs to be adjusted. It may take as long as eight weeks before the full effect of the medication is felt. If the first drug of choice does not help, there may be a waiting period for it to be completely eliminated from the body before a new drug can be started. Many people are tempted to stop taking their medication too soon because they think it is not helping, or because the side effects are too troublesome, or because they feel better and think they do not need it. But even after the person is feeling better, medication must be taken regularly for six to nine months in order to prevent recurrence of the depression. Some medications must be stopped gradually, over a period of time, in order for the body to adjust.

Most antidepressants fall into three main groups. They all affect neurotransmitters, but each affects brain chemistry in slightly different ways and has different side effects.

1. *Tricyclic antidepressants* (e.g., Tofranil and Elavil) came into use in the 1950s, and they are still widely used for severe depression. The term tricyclic refers to the chemical structure of these compounds. They inhibit the reuptake of serotonin and norepinephrine, making more of these neurotransmitters available in the brain. Side effects vary depending on the medication. Some, like Elavil, cause drowsiness, while others may cause restlessness. Other side effects are dry mouth, blurry vision, constipation, difficulty urinating, and weight gain. Not all these medications cause all these problems, and not everyone experiences them. Some of the side effects disappear within a short period of time. Tricyclic antidepressants can cause complications for people with certain kinds of heart disease. The tricyclics also interfere with some medications, including over-the-counter medicines such as antihistamines. Therefore, if you are taking one of these antidepressants, you should not take any other drugs without first consulting your doctor. An overdose of antidepressants can have serious or fatal consequences.

Serena's doctor told her about the possible side effects when she prescribed Elavil and suggested that Serena list them in a notebook so that at the next visit they could discuss any side effects that bothered her. When Serena was told that the drug might cause blurry vision and dry eyes when she used her contact lenses, she was not sure she wanted to take the medicine. Artificial tears to help the dryness and the promise that this problem would disappear in a few weeks helped persuade Serena that these side effects would not be too terrible. The same mechanism that dries the eyes also dries the mouth. Chewing sugarless gum, sucking on sugarless lozenges, and drinking lots of water would help her relieve this side effect. Mild constipation can be relieved by drinking more water and eating more foods high in fiber, such as bran cereal, fruits, and vegetables. Serena's doctor warned her about the possibility of drowsiness from the Elavil but said that the problem of daytime sleepiness could be solved by taking the medication at night. In Serena's case, this side effect would beneficial because one of the symptoms of her depressed state was difficulty falling asleep. The possibility of weight gain was more distressing. The reason for weight gain in some people taking tricyclic antidepressants is not completely understood, but some researchers think it might be due to a craving for carbohydrates as well as a slowing of the metabolism. Serena was horrified at the idea of getting fat, but what were a few pounds compared with the dreadful depression that dominated her life? It turned out that Serena experienced only mild and temporary side effects—dry mouth and eyes—and after a few weeks of taking the prescribed medicine, she felt so well that she wondered why she had ever questioned taking it.

Serious side effects such as fainting, palpitations, vomiting, or excessive drowsiness are not common, but they should be reported to a doctor at once.

2. *MAOIs (Monoamine Oxidase Inhibitors)* were introduced in the 1950s. They inhibit the breakdown of norepinephrine, and they are often helpful in treating the symptoms of atypical depression, such as oversleeping, anxiety, panic attacks, and increased appetite. People on MAOIs must avoid certain foods containing a substance known as tyramine, which is present in some cheeses, wines, and pickles, as well as some medicines. The interaction of tyramine with MAOIs can cause a severe rise in blood pressure that can lead to a stroke or death. People who take MAOIs need to be given a list of all foods and medicines that must be avoided. Your dentist, and other doctors, should also be informed if you are taking this kind of medication. In order to decrease bleeding during a dental procedure, a small amount of epinephrine is often injected along with a local anesthetic such as Novocain. Normally, this causes no problems, but for someone on an MAOI, the epinephrine could cause a severe rise in blood pressure with serious consequences such as stroke.

3. *SSRIs (Selective Serotonin Reuptake Inhibitors)* are the new generation of antidepressants that act on one specific neurotransmitter, serotonin. More than half of all new antidepressant prescriptions written in the United States are for SSRIs.[2] The best known of these is Prozac. Not everyone who suffers from depression is taking Prozac, although it may seem that way. Approved by the FDA in 1988, Prozac was the first of the so-called new generation of antidepressants, and it was proclaimed a wonder drug by the media. Since then, it has been prescribed for more than 40 million people in over one hundred countries, and it is the most widely prescribed antidepressant in the world.[3] But "one size fits all" certainly does not apply here. Prozac is not a miracle cure, nor is it suitable

for everyone with depression. In addition to Prozac, the FDA has approved other similar drugs in this category —Celexa, Luvox, Paxil, and Zoloft—which also act by blocking the reuptake of serotonin. If serotonin alone determined mood, finding the right medicine would be easier than it is. Brain activity may involve about fifty other neurotransmitters that interact with serotonin.[4]

4. *Other New Types.* Two other new antidepressants, Effexor and Serzone, which block the reuptake of both serotonin and norepinephrine, have also been approved by the FDA. Wellbutrin is another antidepressant that is chemically unrelated to the other antidepressants. It has more effect on norepinephrine and dopamine than on serotonin, and it does not seem to cause weight gain. People with eating disorders or those at risk for seizures should not take Wellbutrin.

Although no antidepressant is perfect, the newer antidepressants seem to have less bothersome side effects than earlier drugs; these side effects include nausea, headache, insomnia, and jittery feelings, which are generally temporary. Some antidepressants may cause serious problems when taken with certain other medications. Some people have reported very troublesome side effects during the process of discontinuing use of Paxil, even when the dosage has been decreased very gradually.

CAN ANTIDEPRESSANTS CAUSE VIOLENCE?

Since not all brains are alike, it is not surprising to find that the effects of medication may differ from one person to another. You may have read that antidepressants, and Prozac in particular, may cause violence in a small percentage of the people who take them. Prozac, though recognized as a wonder drug, sometimes appears in headlines as an evil one. Recently, a few reports of violent behavior exhibited by people who happened

A girl kneels before the Columbine Memorial set up after the shootings at Columbine High School in Littleton, Colorado.

to be taking Prozac gained widespread media attention, keeping the issue well publicized. One of the perpetrators of the 1999 tragedy at Littleton, Colorado, in which fifteen people lost their lives, was taking Luvox, a medication similar to Prozac. The idea of a supposed connection between antidepressants and violence has also been promoted by groups opposed to the use of any psychiatric medications. Some studies have shown that a very small group of patients on Prozac may have increased thoughts of suicide, but not everyone accepts these findings.

An FDA advisory committee, an impartial panel of experts, all agreed that there was no evidence of a link between these drugs and violence or suicide. To the contrary, suicidal tendencies decrease when people are treated with antidepressant medications. However, if the drug is not working in an individual case, that person may get worse and show violent or suicidal impulses.[5]

Millions of people have been helped by antidepressants, and adverse reactions are extremely rare. Dr. Peter D. Kramer, author of *Listening to Prozac*, suggests that the energizing effects of the drugs may cause some people to act on fantasies they had not expressed or formulated earlier.[6]

Dr. Peter D. Kramer, author of *Listening to Prozac*.

MEDICATION FOR BIPOLAR DISORDER

Fifteen-year-old Alexis was brought to the emergency room at 3 A.M. because she was threatening to kill her mother. Even though she had not slept for three days, she was full of energy. Earlier in the week, she had started going to school wearing too much makeup and had been dressing in revealing clothes. She acted elated, made embarrassing and inappropriate remarks to teachers and fellow students, and interrupted classes with silly jokes and nonstop talking. Then she began making phone calls to a family friend about investing money in a grandiose and impractical scheme. Alexis became angry when her mother and others tried to calm her down; she had no idea that her judgment was impaired and that her behavior was inappropriate. She thought people were out to get her. Her mother knew that Alexis needed medical help. The psychiatrist made a diagnosis of manic episode and admitted her to the hospital. After thorough interviews and examinations, lithium was prescribed.

Lithium is the most common treatment for bipolar disorder. It diminishes severe manic symptoms within a week or two, but it may take much longer before the condition is fully

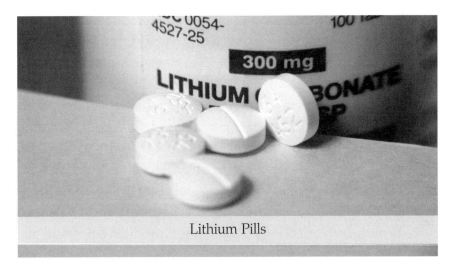

Lithium Pills

controlled. Although Alexis had never had a manic episode before and she had never experienced any period of depression, the psychiatrist told her that depression usually follows or precedes episodes of mania. However, lithium acts to smooth out the mood swings in both directions. Some people have one episode and never experience another, but many have repeated bouts. These people need to keep taking lithium indefinitely. The response to lithium varies, and some individuals are not helped at all.

The difference between an effective dose of lithium and a toxic dose is small, so regular blood tests must be carried out to monitor the amount of drug in the body.

People on lithium may experience side effects such as drowsiness, weakness, nausea, vomiting, hand tremors, or increased thirst and urination, but these side effects usually disappear. Some people gain weight. The drug may also affect kidney and thyroid function.

Anything that lowers the amount of sodium in the body may cause lithium to build up and lead to toxicity. Reducing your salt intake (table salt is sodium chloride), heavy sweating, fever, vomiting, or diarrhea can have this effect. Signs of toxicity include nausea, vomiting, drowsiness, slurred speech, mental dullness, confusion, dizziness, irregular heartbeat, and blurred vision. A serious overdose of lithium can lead to coma and death.

Despite the potential dangers, lithium is a safe and very effective drug when monitored carefully. It enables people to lead normal lives free of disruptive mood swings.

Not everyone with bipolar disorder responds to lithium, and some cannot take it because of pre-existing thyroid, kidney, or heart disorders. Fortunately, other medications are available. Anti-seizure drugs such as Tegretol and Depakote have been found effective in controlling mood swings and are widely used.

DO KIDS NEED PROZAC?

The number of children taking psychiatric drugs has risen sharply, creating great concern among doctors, because not enough is known about the drugs' effects on young brains.[7] Many experts believe the drugs are used more widely than necessary. How often are drugs prescribed to children and teens who are suffering from the pangs of growing up? How often are other ailments confused with depression and bipolar disease? Many children with depression also suffer from attention deficit disorder, conduct disorder, obsessive-compulsive disorder, or learning disabilities.

Questions still remain about how to treat young people with bipolar and major depressive disorders. In the last few years, however, the National Institute of Mental Health has been funding studies at medical centers around the country in which researchers are investigating the usefulness of various drugs and psychotherapy in children and adolescents. They want to find out how well lithium and other mood-stabilizing drugs work and what the long-term effects are in young people with bipolar disorder. Some studies have shown that some of the newer antidepressant medications, the SSRIs, are safe and effective for the short-term treatment of young people with severe and persistent depression. The experts have also concluded that the tricyclic antidepressants are not as effective or as safe for young people, and so they do not support their use.[8]

Correct diagnosis is important because using the wrong medication may create worse problems. As noted earlier, stimulants such as Ritalin, which are often prescribed for ADHD, may worsen manic symptoms when given to children with bipolar disorder. Similarly, using antidepressants to treat a child who has bipolar disorder may also trigger manic symptoms.

Parents can contact the National Institute of Mental Health (NIMH), the National Alliance for the Mentally Ill (NAMI), or other organizations listed at the end of this book for help in finding a psychiatrist who has had experience in treating these disorders.

CAN HERBAL TREATMENT HELP DEPRESSION?

St. John's Wort, an herbal remedy sold over the counter, appears to help some mildly depressed people, but a new study finds it useless against major forms of depression.[9] St. John's Wort is a common plant that grows wild, and extracts from it are widely sold in health food stores as a nutritional supplement. Since it is not regulated as a drug by the U.S. Food and Drug Administration, each brand may contain a varying amount of the active ingredients. No one knows which of the numerous chemicals in the herb are the active ingredients or what the right dose is.

Bottle of St. John's Wort, an herbal remedy to help combat depression

"Natural" substances can have harmful side effects, especially if taken in large quantities or with other substances. St. John's Wort interacts with prescription drugs such as blood thinners and birth control pills. It also reduces the effectiveness of the drug Indinavir, which is used to fight HIV/AIDS.

Due to considerable public interest in the United States, the National Institute of Mental Health is carrying out a study on St. John's Wort at thirteen university-affiliated mental health clinics around the country. Many scientists are concerned that some of the 1.5 million people in the United States who use it regularly might be at risk for suicide, a risk that might be prevented by taking prescription drugs instead.[10] A report on April 18, 2001 indicated that St. John's Wort was not helpful in treating depression.[11] Doctors recommend that people suffering from depression take antidepressants rather than St. John's Wort since their chances of improvement are far greater with drugs than with an herbal remedy.

SAM-e is a natural substance that has become popular in the battle against depression. Some doctors believe it is a medical marvel that treats depression in half the time of prescription drugs, with virtually no side effects. SAM-e is an over-the-counter, natural supplement. According to the book, *Stop Depression Now*, SAM-e has helped alleviate the depression of hundreds of people around the world.[12] Considerable success with SAM-e has been reported in Europe, but manufacture of this drug is not regulated in the United States, so the active content may vary. Although SAM-e has indeed shown some promise, more research is needed before it can be recommended as an alternative to antidepressants.[13] Depression is a serious disease that is best treated by a doctor.

ELECTROSHOCK THERAPY

Electroshock therapy, also known as electroconvulsive therapy or ECT, is useful for individuals whose depression is severe and life-threatening and who cannot take antidepressant medication because of a medical risk. It is most commonly used in cases where antidepressant medications do not provide sufficient relief of symptoms.

ECT has had a bad name, but that is changing. In the film *One Flew Over the Cuckoo's Nest*, electroshock therapy and lobotomy turn a patient into a zombie. (Lobotomy is an operation in which some brain tissue is deliberately destroyed. This procedure is no longer used as a treatment for depression.) The modern version of ECT is nothing like the torture shown in some movies. In the movies, large amounts of electric current are applied to patients who are completely awake, causing violent seizures throughout the body. In reality, it is no longer a bone-breaking, memory-modifying, fearsome treatment.

The stigma attached to ECT was greater a few decades ago than it is today. In 1972, vice presidential candidate Thomas Eagleton withdrew from politics after it was revealed that he had received ECT for depression. The stigma at that time was so great that many people incorrectly felt this treatment would diminish Eagleton's ability to serve as a high public official. Today the outcome after ECT is recognized as good, and many people are now willing to admit how much it has helped them. Some famous people, such as TV commentator Dick Cavett and Roland Kohloff, a tympanist with the New York Philharmonic Orchestra, are among those who acknowledge successful experiences with ECT.[15] Despite the good results in some cases, research has suggested that without follow-up medication, 84 percent of the patients treated with ECT became depressed again within six months.

Some severely depressed, psychotic adolescents have been safely treated with ECT where other methods have failed. It has also been used successfully on a few children suffering from overwhelming impulses to mutilate

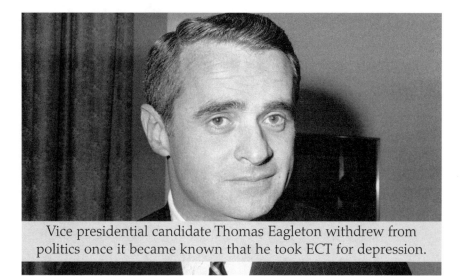

Vice presidential candidate Thomas Eagleton withdrew from politics once it became known that he took ECT for depression.

themselves and on children who have severe mental retardation.[16] But no one knows exactly why ECT works. Does it interfere with the growth and development of the brain? ECT is generally not considered a good treatment choice for young children or teens, and it is rarely used for them because of the fear that repeated seizures might damage a young brain.

TV personality Dick Cavett had a positive experience with ECT.

New techniques for ECT have vastly improved the treatment. Patients are given anesthesia, and vital functions are carefully monitored in the operating room. While the patient is asleep, a muscle relaxant is administered, and a low-energy current is passed through the brain to stimulate a brief, mild seizure. The patient is not aware of this part of the actual treatment. Within minutes after the treatment, the patient is awake. The side effects are some confusion and memory loss; they are usually temporary but some people report lasting problems. For full benefits, three sessions of ECT per week for several weeks are required.[14] The treatment continues to be controversial, with some specialists and patients praising it and others believing it causes brain damage. Many patients who suffer severely from depression and manic depression feel that the treatment is worth the risk.

PSYCHOTHERAPY

Antidepressants can help to correct the imbalance of chemicals in the brain, but they cannot undo the suffering caused by emotional imbalance. In some cases, psychotherapy works almost as well as medication alone, provided that symptoms are mild to moderate. Many studies have demonstrated that the combination of medication and therapy produces the best outcome.

One effective and widely used type of therapy for depression is called *cognitive therapy*. This is talk therapy based on the idea that depressed people have a distorted view of themselves, the world, and the future. They think they are worthless, they feel helpless and hopeless, and believe that the world is a hostile place. If you are depressed, you may have developed a negative pattern of thinking without realizing it.

Eliot felt that he was responsible for his parents' divorce, for his sister's leukemia, and for every bad thing that happened to him. Certain that nothing would turn out right, he stopped participating in sports, he let his school work slide, and he stopped seeing his friends. He became more and more depressed until he began seeing a psychiatrist who worked with him using cognitive therapy. After many discussions, Eliot began to identify his distorted thinking and counteract his pessimistic outlook. He learned to put things in perspective and to understand that he was not responsible for many of the negative aspects of life.

Behavioral therapy is similar to cognitive therapy in that it teaches people to alter their thought patterns, but it also helps them change their behavior. Interpersonal therapy, which focuses on the development and improvement of relationships, is also used to treat depression. In *psychodynamic therapy* people explore their past for unresolved emotional conflicts. This therapy helps people understand themselves, identify their feelings, and cope with their conflicts.

Recent research has shown that short-term psychotherapy, especially cognitive-behavioral therapy, can help relieve depression in children and adolescents. Parents need to get support as well, to help their children and the rest of the family deal with the illness. Medication alone is not enough; everyone with emotional problems needs support.

EXERCISE FOR MILD DEPRESSION

If you are feeling down or blue, does your mood lift if you work up a sweat riding your mountain bike, playing basketball, or going for a run? Regular aerobic exercise has been shown to help people with mild depression. Just taking a brisk walk or a swim for thirty minutes three times a week can help to release the same brain chemicals that are affected by antidepressants. The famous "runner's high" experienced by serious joggers is the result of an increase in serotonin in the brain.

Exercise alone has not been shown to be successful in treating cases of severe depression, but some researchers believe that exercise along with medication works well in helping people deal with mild depression and keeping the condition from returning.

Exercise has been shown to help people cope with depression.

DEPRESSION IS TREATABLE

Finding the right treatment is not always easy, but depression CAN be treated, and most people feel better with just a few weeks or months of treatment. In addition to your doctor, you may want to contact some of the organizations listed at the end of this book.

NOTES

1. Depression, National Institute of Mental Health, www.nimh.nih.gov/depression/index.htm
2. William S. Appleton, *Prozac and the New Antidepressants* (New York: Plume Books, Penguin Putnam, 2000), p. 52.
3. http://www. prozac.com/home2.htm
4. Appleton, p. 50.
5. Andrew L. Morrison, M.D., *The Antidepressant Sourcebook* (New York: Main Street Books, Doubleday, 1999), pp. 55, 56.
6. Peter D. Kramer, *Listening to Prozac* (New York: Viking, 1993), p. 306.
7. Erica Goode, "Sharp Rise Found In Psychiatric Drugs for the Very Young," *New York Times*, February 23, 2000.
8. http://www.nimh.nih.gov/publicat/depchildresfact.cfm
9. http://www.nimh.nih.gov/publicat/stjohnqa.htm
10. Richard Brown and others, *Stop Depression Now* (New York: Putnam, 1999), jacket flap.
11. Denise Grady, "Study Finds Herbal Remedy Useless Against Depression," *New York Times*, April 18, 2001.
12. *SAM-e for Depression* (Boston, MA: The Harvard Mental Health Letter, January 2001): 5.
13. http://www.nimh.nih.gov/publicat/depression.cfm
14. http://www.nimh.nih.gov/publicat/depresfact.cfm
15. wysiwyg://10/http://healthexcite.com/topics_content/dmk/dmk_article_5963105.
16. wysiwyg://123http://wwww.intelihealth.com...EMIHC000/333/7228/298506.html?k=basePrint

Chapter Six

FAMOUS PEOPLE

Has a "black dog" ever shadowed you? What did you do and how did you feel when you couldn't shake it? Winston Churchill was one of many famous and successful people, past and present, who have been followed by the black dog. Each person's depression feels different, but no one is immune. Astronaut Buzz Aldrin, actress Patty Duke, musician Lou Reed, Olympic athlete Greg Louganis, journalist Mike Wallace, and former First Lady Barbara Bush are only a few among countless numbers of famous people from all walks of life who have suffered from depression. You can find some of these people on a Web page listing the names of living celebrities who have publicly stated that they have experienced severe depression. The purpose of the Web page is to provide inspiration for others with depression.[1] Many famous people from the past are also known to have suffered from depression, and they, too, are individuals from every profession. Here are a few of these achievers.

WINSTON CHURCHILL

Winston Churchill was prime minister of Great Britain during World War II, and he was well known as a forceful, tireless, courageous man and great leader who inspired the British during the most perilous days of the war. According to psychiatrist Anthony Storr, Churchill was able to persuade others that despair could be overcome because he had battled

Winston Churchill

despair all his life.[2] He may have been one of those people for whom depression is a spur to great achievement. In order to avoid falling into an overwhelming state of depression, such people push themselves relentlessly with tremendous energy. Like several of his ancestors, Churchill was prone to wide swings of mood, alternating between periods of great energy and depression. Churchill suffered from recurrent fits of depression all his life but was successful in conquering the black dog until a few years before his death at age 90.

ABRAHAM LINCOLN

Abraham Lincoln's depression is more commonly recognized than that of many other famous people. He probably suffered from manic-depressive disorder, for he had periods of melancholy alternating with wild, talkative periods. However, his depressed moods seemed to be predominant.

Abraham Lincoln

At the age of 29, Lincoln plunged into a deep depression, which, according to some accounts, was the result of the death of Ann Rutledge, his first love. Although grief and depression are normal upon the loss of a loved one, Lincoln's depression was more profound and long lasting. At one point, his friends took away his knives and razors for fear he might commit suicide.

Lincoln later fell in love with Mary Todd but failed to show up on the day of their wedding. His friends found him walking alone at daybreak, restless and seriously depressed. They watched him day and night because they feared he would commit suicide. Lincoln is believed to have contemplated suicide on a number of other occasions.

As treatment for his nervous condition, Lincoln was taking a medication known as "Blue Mass" for depression.

This was a common treatment in the 1850s. The ingredients for "Blue Mass" were licorice root, honey, sugar, rose water, rose petals, and mercury. Lincoln may have had a daily dose of over 9,000 times the amount of mercury that is now considered a safe daily dose. Some of the symptoms of mercury poisoning are aggressive behavior and mood swings, so some historians wonder if mercury may have been responsible for these symptoms in Lincoln[3]. Psychiatrist Dr. Ronald Fieve suggests that Lincoln probably would have responded well to modern drug treatment. However, if he had taken such a treatment, the weight of public opinion would probably have ruled him out as a presidential candidate, as it did Senator Thomas Eagleton so many years later.[4]

THEODORE ROOSEVELT

While Lincoln's moods were mostly low, the moods of the twenty-sixth president of the United States were mainly high. Theodore Roosevelt was very charismatic, and his high spirits were reflected in the mood of the country. He was very energetic and talked a great deal. His impatience and tendency to get excited interfered with his career as a young politician at first. However, his charm helped him to "rise like a rocket," which were the words he used in describing his career. Roosevelt appears to have suffered periods of melancholy, but he surrendered to depression for only short periods.

Roosevelt was a generally happy manic, but he sometimes became irritable, and newspapers reported his violent quarrels. As police commissioner of New York City, he used some of his manic energy in walking the streets at night checking on patrol officers. He would return to his office couch for a few hours of sleep and be ready to deal with the world at ten in the morning. This inexhaustible energy is typical of the manic.

Theodore Roosevelt

Roosevelt is best known for his action in the Spanish-American War. As commander of a cavalry regiment called the Rough Riders, he was deeply loved by his men, and he led them with great enthusiasm on a famous charge in the battle of San Juan Hill.

Roosevelt's energy also played a major part in his tenure as governor of New York and later as president of the United States. But he occasionally got too enthusiastic and exhibited manic rage, bullying people, distorting facts, and contradicting himself. His friends were aware that his energy level was dangerously high and that his judgment was impaired; one politician, in fact, referred to him as a madman. Roosevelt used some of his boundless energy to write an estimated 18 million words over the course of his life. One hundred thousand of his letters have been preserved; a collection of his writings, including books, articles, and speeches, totals twenty volumes.

Roosevelt's mood swings are believed to have ultimately played a part in his failure to be renominated for president. Even so, he is still considered one of the United States' greatest politicians.[5]

ISAAC NEWTON

The English mathematician and physicist Sir Isaac Newton was one of the world's greatest geniuses. He was just in his early twenties in the middle of the seventeenth century when he made his major contributions to science. He formulated the basic laws of mechanics, he invented calculus, and he made the discovery for which he is most famous—the law of gravitation.

Perhaps you have a classmate who acts the way Newton did: He spent more time making mechanical models than playing with his schoolmates, and he was not very well liked. As a young adult, he was a loner; he was described as a typical absent-minded scholar who became so involved with his studies that he sometimes forgot to eat. He was touchy and overly sensitive. He was obsessed with a sense of guilt; he expressed feelings of worthlessness, and he never seemed to be able to enjoy himself.

At age 50, Newton experienced what appeared to be a psychotic episode. He accused his friends of plotting against him, and he showed symptoms of depression. He recovered from his depression, and although he did not make any scientific discoveries as great as those he had achieved during his youth, he remained productive and lived to the age of 85.

Isaac Newton

Newton's father died before he was born, and when he was 3 years old, his mother remarried and abandoned little Isaac to the care of his grandmother. After the death of his stepfather, his mother returned with the children of her second marriage. Newton evidently was unable to get over his feelings of resentment at having been abandoned. Anthony Storr suggests this early experience may have contributed to his depressive personality and his distrust of other people. In addition to his great genius, part of his achievement may be traced to his need to gain self-esteem through his work. Storr comments that although Newton may have felt he was worthless as a person, his work would bring him fame and admiration that he could not gain in other ways.[6]

Suppose Newton had taken antidepressant medication that helped lift his mood. Do you think he would have been so driven to achieve? Or would he have achieved even more than he did?

DEPRESSION AND CREATIVITY

From early times, people thought that madness and genius were linked. The ancient Greeks believed that artistic inspiration was a gift of the gods. Aristotle noted that all men who were outstanding in philosophy, poetry, and the arts were melancholic.[7]

In her book *Touched with Fire*, Kay Redfield Jamison discusses the relationship between the artistic temperament and manic-depressive illness, drawing examples from the lives of artists, writers, and composers. She notes that compared with the general population, artists and writers have a higher rate of manic-depressive or depressive illness.[8] However, not all successful writers and artists suffer from mood disorders.

In her study of writers and artists, Jamison found that most of them had experienced intense, very productive episodes during which they were full of energy, enthusiasm, and confidence, and their thoughts flowed freely. Most believed that their intense moods were necessary and important to their work. Jamison notes that individuals with this kind of temperament may be more likely to choose artistic careers. The characteristics of the hypomania of manic depression are similar to those of creative thought. But the intense moods and other qualities that appear to be the same in the personalities of artists and in people with mood disorders may not be identical.

Although the high mood phase of manic depression may help an artist's creative process, if it progresses too far the individual can no longer think coherently. Similarly, no artist can be creative if he or she is paralyzed by depression or is psychotic. As poet Robert Lowell observed, depression is no gift from the Muse.[9]

But mild depression can enhance artistic productivity because it is accompanied by introspection, brooding, and self-searching, and it can produce poetic and philosophical insights. Some research has indicated that people in a mildly depressed state have a more objective and clearer view of reality than people with normal mood states.[10]

One study of fifteen mid-twentieth-century artists found that four of the artists suffered bouts of extreme depression and two others suffered a milder form of depression. Two committed suicide and two died in car crashes that may have reflected the intent of suicide.[11]

Not all artists and creative people suffer from depression, but the famous people described here, and many more, were able to accomplish great things either in spite of it or because of it.

CREATIVE PEOPLE AND DEPRESSION

Composers who suffered from depression include Irving Berlin, Robert Schumann, George Frederick Handel, Hector Berlioz, Gustav Mahler, Cole Porter, Sergey Rachmaninoff, and Peter Tschaikovsky. Writers who had mood disorders include Hans Christian Andersen, F. Scott Fitzgerald, Ernest Hemingway, Hermann Hesse, Charles Dickens, Ralph Waldo Emerson, Victor Hugo, Eugene O'Neill, Robert Louis Stevenson, Leo Tolstoy, and Tennessee Williams. Robert Burns, Samuel Taylor Coleridge, Emily Dickinson, T.S Eliot, Oliver Goldsmith, John Keats, Robert Lowell, Edna St. Vincent Millay, Sylvia Plath, Edgar Allan Poe, Ezra Pound, Anne Sexton, Percy Bysshe Shelley, Alfred Lord Tennyson, Dylan Thomas, and Walt Whitman are included in a long list of poets who suffered from depression.[12]

NOTES

1. www.frii.com/~parrot/living.html, Famous People Who Have Experienced Depression or Manic Depression.
2. Anthony Storr, *Churchill's Black Dog, Kafka's Mice, and Other Phenomena of the Human Mind.* (New York: Grove Press, 1988), p. 5.
3. wyswyg://7/.http://sleepdisorders.about.com/library/weekly/aa072301a.htm.
4. Ronald R. Fieve, *Moodswing: The Third Revolution in Psychiatry* (New York: William Morrow, 1975), p. 124.
5. Ibid., p. 125.
6. Storr, *Churchill's Black Dog*, pp. 83–103.
7. Ibid., p. 51.
8. Kay Redfield Jamison, *Touched with Fire: Manic-Depressive Illness and the Artistic Temperament* (New York: Free Press, 1996), p. 5.
9. Ibid., p. 117.
10. Ibid., p.119.
11. http://users.lycaeum.org/martins/m2/creativ2.html
12. www.psych.helsinki.fi/~janne/asdfaq/49.html

Chapter Seven

WHEN A FRIEND IS DEPRESSED

Do you have a friend who is depressed? If you do not have one now, the chances are likely that you will in the future. Will you know how to help your friend? Many families and friends of people with depression want to help but don't know how to start. When a friend seems to be hurting and no one can figure out why, depression may be the culprit. Depression may masquerade as substance abuse, stomach pain, unexplained fatigue, or many other conditions, and only a professional can sort this out.

Depression may not be recognized even when it happens close to home. This was the case in one family where the father had committed suicide and the son was showing unrecognized signs of depression. The boy killed himself on the anniversary of the father's suicide, and it was not until then that the family learned that both father and son were depressed. While he was alive, the family thought the father was just angry and irritable. Sadly, treatment could have helped both father and son.

If you are depressed, your friends can offer wonderful support. Depression may make it difficult to make a bed or even to put the toothpaste on a brush. Making a phone call to a doctor might be something you just can't do without the help of a friend.

Alysha said she was depressed because she could not get tickets for a show. Brandon thought a movie was depressing.

Vera felt depressed when she came away from the nursing home because her mother complained during every visit. But all these people only felt depressed for a short time. In contrast, Alexis was profoundly depressed. She suffered from sleeping and eating problems, feelings of hopelessness and helplessness, and an inability to enjoy life. These symptoms were not fleeting; they continued for more than two weeks and constituted major depression. She needed medical help and a friend to give her support after she finally obtained professional help.

RECOGNIZING DEPRESSION IN A FRIEND

Although you need a doctor's help in diagnosing depression, you may be able to tell if your friends need help by checking the following symptoms, especially if they last longer than two weeks.

Look for feelings of:

Sadness or emptiness

Hopelessness, pessimism, or guilt

Helplessness or worthlessness

Do your friends seem:

Unable to make decisions?

Unable to concentrate and remember?

To have lost interest or pleasure in ordinary activities, like sports or band or talking on the phone?

To have more problems with school or family?

Do they complain of:

Loss of energy and drive?

Trouble falling asleep, staying asleep, or getting up?

Appetite problems? Are they losing or gaining weight?

Headaches, stomachaches, or backaches?

Chronic aches and pains in muscles or joints?

Has their behavior changed suddenly so that:

They are restless or more irritable?

They want to be alone most of the time?

They've started cutting classes or dropped hobbies and activities?

You think they may be drinking heavily or taking other drugs?

Have they talked about:

Death?

Suicide?

If you answered yes to several of these questions, encourage your friends to seek help from a doctor, parent, or teacher. Get help immediately from an adult you trust if any friend mentions death or suicide.[1]

WHAT CAN YOU SAY?

If you have a friend who is depressed, you may be tempted to say, "It's just a phase," or to ask, "Why should you be sad?" These are the wrong comments to make about a treatable disease that cannot be willed away.

Just as other organs of the body may fail, the brain, too, can malfunction. The most important action you can take to help a depressed person is to lead him or her to professional treatment. However, there are some words that depressed people have reported as helpful.

Start by finding a calm, quiet time when you can talk to your friend. Perhaps you can invite your friend to share a soda and a snack with you at home or in a favorite place. Express your concern about changes in the person's behavior. Then you can say some of the following:

"I know you are hurting."

"Depression really sucks. It must really tick you off."

"The chemicals in your brain may be out of sync. There is medicine for that."

"Tell me about how you feel. Maybe I can think of something to help you."

"You can always cry on my shoulder."

"You are important to me."

"Don't think you are weak. You have a common disease."

"I'm here for you."

"You can get beyond this downer."

WHAT CAN YOU DO?

Suggest some ways to find help. A family doctor, a religious leader, a school counselor, or a teacher may be able to refer the friend to a professional. (See other resources on page 105.)

Continue to care about your friend who has a common, treatable disease.

Encourage your friend to stick with his or her medicine and/or therapy.

Give emotional support by listening carefully, making frequent eye contact.

Be optimistic and offer hope. "With help, things will seem better."

Invite your friend to join you in activities he or she used to enjoy, but don't push too hard.

Remember that depression is not a weakness.

Avoid being judgmental.

THE WORST THINGS TO SAY

"Stop feeling sorry for yourself."

"You have great stuff, why aren't you happy?"

"You don't want to be happy."

"You need to get high."

"You should stop taking all that medicine."

"Everybody has a bad day now and then."

SUPPORT GROUPS

You can help a friend by encouraging him or her to join a support group. Support groups help the depressed person to follow a treatment plan, and they also provide a place where people with depression are accepted and understood. They help patients to understand that depressive disorders do not define who you are. They give them a chance to learn from the experiences of other people who have "been there."

You can locate a support group for your friend by calling the National Depressive and Manic-Depressive Association (NDMDA) at 1-800-826-3632. This organization has 275 local chapters and support groups. Each offers at least one support group where people can privately share their feelings and ask questions. They may also help family members or loved ones of people with depression. Many chapters of the group have medical advisors and appointed leaders.

Support groups provide strong allies in the fight against depression.

ACTIVITIES FOR MILD DEPRESSION

If your friend is mildly depressed, you may wish to suggest some activities.

As noted earlier, exercise alone cannot successfully treat cases of severe depression, but regular aerobic exercise has been shown to help people with mild depression by increasing serotonin in the brain. A routine exercise program will help to keep a person upbeat.

Reaching out to other people helps to prevent mildly depressed people from dwelling on their feelings. Join your friend in volunteering to sing with people in a nursing home, push wheelchairs, arrange flowers or read to patients. Working in a soup kitchen, tutoring at a local school, and other such activities can also be antidotes to negative feelings.

Gardening, woodworking, knitting or needlepoint, or indulging in some other favorite hobby can improve one's mood.

Suggest your friend keep a journal. Putting feelings on paper helps to release anger and depressed feelings in many people. For some, it is helpful to write about thoughts and emotions in ways that will enable them to make sense of their experiences and identify ways to resolve conflicts. Although studies have indicated that expressive writing helps some people to bolster their mood, for others there is no improvement or even negative results.[2]

Help your friend to go on-line. Keeping in touch with family and friends with e-mail and exploring the Internet can help relieve depression.

Listening to music or playing an instrument helps to boost moods. Rhythmic sounds appear to have a spontaneous effect on neural mechanisms. Music has been shown to reduce depression. The kind of music people prefer, anything from heavy metal to Bach, can have a positive effect.[3]

Dance therapy may also help to elevate mood. The effects of dance therapy may be short-lived, but it can be especially helpful as a mood elevator while one is waiting for antidepressants to begin to work.

BEING A FRIEND

Just being a friend is an important way to help someone who is depressed. Some people report feeling strange around friends who are taking medicine for depression and/or seeing a therapist. You should admire these people for dealing with their problems, and you should know that there is a good chance that they will feel better as a result.

NOTES

1. http:www.nimh.nih.gov/publicat/friend/cfm
2. Simeon Margolis and Karen L. Swartz, *Depression and Anxiety* (Baltimore, MD: Johns Hopkins, 2000), p. 37.
3. Ibid., pp. 36–37.

Chapter Eight

TEEN SUICIDE: WARNINGS, CAUSES, AND PREVENTION

IF YOU FEEL SUICIDAL: READ THIS FIRST

If you feel suicidal, it does not mean that you are a weak or a bad person. It doesn't even mean you really want to die. It means your pain is deep and you do not know a good way to cope with it. When you feel this way, please call a local crisis line. You will find one in your phone book. If you cannot, ask a friend, a teacher, a doctor, or someone you trust to help you find one, or you should seek help from a professional caregiver. There are people out there who will be with you on the phone or in person at this terrible time. They will care for you without judging you. They will care about you. Call someone at a suicide hotline listed below.

If you cannot call someone now and you are feeling suicidal, give yourself some distance by waiting twenty-four hours before you do anything to harm yourself. Put some distance between your suicidal feelings and suicidal action.

When people react badly to your suicidal ideas, it is probably because they are frightened or angry. When they say or do thoughtless things, it is about their own fears, not about you.

In an emergency dial 911.

The Covenant House Nineline (1-800-999-9999) provides counseling nationwide and may be able to locate a crisis service near you.

Someone may be trying to take his or her life at this very moment. A suicidal person is one whose pain exceeds his or her coping resources. For this person, suicide offers relief from pain. They may be suffering too much to see that there is another way out. They cannot find another way to reduce the pain or increase their coping resources.

Every day approximately 86 Americans commit suicide, and many of them are teens.[1] No one knows how many more people attempt suicide, but it has been estimated that for every death from suicide, eight to twenty-five attempts are made.[2] Over the last decade, the suicide rate in young people has increased dramatically.[3] It is now four times that of the 1950 rate.[4]

Suicide is the third leading cause of death among Americans 15 to 24 years old, exceeded only by accidental injury and homicide.[5] There is a good chance that most of these suicides could have been prevented. Hotline workers are trained to say the right things to those who call, so making people aware of those workers is an important kind of prevention. Saying the right thing to a friend, as suggested later in this chapter, and reporting threats to adults who know how to help are important ways to stop someone from suicide. Many suicidal individuals are experiencing a chemical imbalance in their brains due to depression. Getting help for a friend's depression after the immediate threat of suicide is over is another way to prevent suicide.

A WARNING CAN BE MISSED

Almost all teens who commit suicide leave a trail of warnings. Recognizing these warnings is an important part of prevention. Darcy's mother did not recognize her call for help. The music coming from her room was always loud, and it upset her mother, who worked as an editor in a home office. Darcy's mother asked her to turn down the volume again and again. One night when her mother was under the pressure of a deadline, she screamed at Darcy to lower the noise level. Darcy replied, "It will soon be very quiet in here. You won't hear any more noise." Her mother went back to reading a manuscript, thinking Darcy was going to bed. Darcy did go to bed after she flipped the switches on her equipment. Then she took a large dose of pills that she had placed next to her bed. She never woke up. After the funeral, Darcy's mother dwelled on the words, "It will soon be very quiet in here." Some nights she played loud music and pretended Darcy was still there. She had so utterly missed a warning.

Even professionals can miss warning signs. This was the case with Vance. Vance's father was an alcoholic who became violent and physically abusive toward Vance and Vance's mother when he was drunk. When he sobered up and realized how much damage he had done, he would always be very sorry. As a result, Vance's mother felt she could not call for help. Each time her husband beat her and Vance, she believed him when he said he would not do it again. Vance grew more withdrawn and depressed and was afraid to ask anyone for help for fear his father's problems would be uncovered. He tried to relieve his pain with drugs, but he was caught buying and selling heroin to pay for his habit and had to spend some time in jail. When he was released, he was too embarrassed to return to school. He tried to find a job but had no success. He felt worthless and helpless. With help from a social worker, Vance managed to rent a small apartment, where he would ostensibly begin life anew. Actually, Vance wanted to get out of the house so he could take his life without making a mess. He seemed happy about the new apartment, but the happiness was not real. Two days after he moved in, he cut his wrists in the bathroom. He left a note for his mother:

"I owe the happiness in my life to you. I have no future and I can't go on any longer. I moved so you would not have to clean up the mess after I died. Please give my dog to your cousin. Love, Vance."

After Vance died, the social worker who had helped him find an apartment was very upset. She said she should have realized that his sudden calmness was a sign that he had made a decision to die.

WARNING SIGNS YOU SHOULD KNOW

Would you know what to say if you recognized some danger signals in a friend? Would you know the warning signs that can be thinly veiled as questions about a third person? Most people who are thinking of suicide reveal their thoughts directly or indirectly, giving parents or friends a chance to direct them to someone who can help. Many school counselors, crisis center hotline workers, doctors, social workers, priests, ministers, and rabbis are trained to help or can direct someone who is suicidal to professional help.

Untreated depression is the number one cause of suicide. If you know someone who is depressed, it is especially important to watch carefully for the following warning signals of suicide. About 90 percent of all suicides are diagnosable as depressed.[6]

Preoccupation with death: Questions about the hereafter, talk about another person's suicide, interest in recurrent death themes in music, drawings, or literature.

A settling of affairs: More than normal concern about a will, life insurance, and other documents.

Giving away prized possessions: An especially important signal when the person is young.

Statements about hopelessness, worthlessness, or helplessness: "You would be better off without me." "I can't do anything right; life is useless." "I wish I could just disappear."

Unusual visiting or phoning of people who are loved: Saying goodbye in anticipation of planned suicide without actually explaining why they are visiting or calling.

Talking or joking about suicide: A way of getting your reaction to the subject.

Obsession with guns or knives: A depressed person thinking about suicide may be drawn to objects of destruction.

Self-destructive behavior: Self-injury, alcohol or other drug abuse, or self-mutilation may be a call for help.

Close calls with death: Several single-person accidents, reckless driving, and walking in front of traffic may be signs of suicide attempts. People who aren't ready to take their lives may tempt fate this way.

Suddenly happier and calmer tone in someone who has been seriously depressed: The person may seem peaceful because the conflict of whether or not to die has been resolved.

Changes in appearance: The person no longer cares about upkeep of clothing or hair.

Any of these danger signs may mean that a person is focusing on death as a way of easing the pain of depression or another problem.

AT RISK FOR SUICIDE

Knowing who is at risk for suicide is another important part of prevention. As mentioned earlier, people with major depression are at high risk for suicide. Within five years of suffering a depression, an estimated 25 percent try to kill themselves.[7]

Teens who come from homes where someone has attempted or committed suicide are high on the list of those at risk. The danger is especially great on the anniversary of a close family member's suicide. Exactly one year after a man took his own life by falling in front of a train, his lover followed the same pattern. In some cases of "anniversary suicide," people may be attempting to join those they love.

It may be that the first suicide lowers the restraints against this kind of act. Soon after a person commits suicide, there may be a rash of them in the same community, for local suicides may have a contagious influence. The suicide of celebrities or peers may also precipitate similar actions.

People who have already attempted suicide are at risk for future attempts. Many of them, especially those whose problems have not been solved, repeat their attempts, unconsciously hoping that their cry for help will be heard this time.

Substance abusers are at risk for suicide because their usual sense of self-protection may not be functioning and their judgment may be clouded. They may not realize that their depression is drug induced. Tom, for example, smoked crack whenever he could get it. He experienced cycles of highs and lows, but during one of his depressed periods he smashed his car into a pole in an effort to take his life. In periods when he was not using drugs, Tom was an excellent lawyer. Routine use of many drugs can promote depression and suicidal thoughts.

Suicide and attempted suicide are five to twenty times higher among abusers of alcohol and other drugs than among the general population.[8] Few drug abusers realize that their depression may be drug related and that their drugged feelings do not reflect the way things really are.

Gays, gifted people under pressure to perform perfectly, those who are abused, and other teens who suffer from special problems may be at *very* high risk if a second problem is added to one that already makes life difficult. Suppose a friend who is depressed suffers from a traumatic experience such as loss of a parent, separation of parents, an unwanted pregnancy, or a move to a strange place. This extra pressure may tip the scales toward suicide, making it seem like the only answer.

Some triggering events may not appear to be important to older adults, but to teens they may seem huge. To many teens, it seems impossible to fail without being a failure. Immediate feelings block their ability to see reasonable solutions to their lives on a long-term basis. Experts say that the urge to die lasts about fifteen minutes. Many teens who kill themselves do so with a gun found at home. If a gun kept at home is hidden, or unloaded with the bullets hidden separately, a teen may make it past that time.[9] Easy access to lethal methods definitely plays a part in suicide.

WHAT CAN YOU SAY OR DO?

Not everyone who is depressed is suicidal, but it is wise to ask the person if you think this might be the case. If you have *any* reason to suspect your friend might be considering suicide, ask him or her. There is some stigma attached to the subject of suicide, so your friend might be relieved to know that you feel comfortable discussing the subject and that you are willing to take the problem seriously. Then listen and listen some more.

If the answer to your question about suicide is yes, ask if the friend has a plan for how to do it. You can probably find out if it is an emergency situation by asking when it will happen.

Usually, three criteria can show how serious a person is about committing suicide:

Having a plan.

Having the resources to carry out the act or means of obtaining them.

Being ready to carry out the action.

A person may commit suicide even without a definite plan. If you have any clues that a suicide is imminent, even if the person has no exact plan, you should contact your local emergency room. Someone there will be able to make a professional judgment about what to do next. If this is not helpful, try a suicide crisis line mentioned on page 105 or check your local phone book under mental health, social services, or hotlines.

If you are not with the suicidal person but you learn about the situation by phone or e-mail, make arrangements for someone to go to the friend and stay there until help arrives. Someone may have to take your friend to the nearest clinic or hospital emergency room.

WHAT NOT TO SAY OR DO

Don't challenge the person by saying, "Go ahead and do it."

Don't try to argue the person out of feeling suicidal.

Don't assume that the person is just trying to get attention by threatening suicide.

Don't say "snap out of it," "get it together," "don't do such a dumb thing," or something of that sort.

Don't give false reassurances.

Don't ignore the warning signs.

<u>DON'T KEEP THE THREAT A SECRET!</u> This is one time when a secret *should* be shared with a doctor or another professional. This situation is not a test of friendship but a response to an illness. You may save a life.

Do not abandon the person after professional help has begun.

IF A SUICIDE HAPPENS

If you do not succeed in preventing the suicide, do not feel guilty. It is not your fault. Some people are so determined to kill themselves that no one can prevent it. Repeating to yourself that you did the best you could and are not responsible for your friend's death may help.

You may feel a mixture of emotions if the person was your friend. The stages of grief are denial, depression, anger, bargaining, and acceptance, but no one goes through these stages in exactly the same way. In the case of suicide, the grief process also includes feelings of failure, guilt, shame, and rejection toward the person who committed suicide as well as toward yourself, or even God. The mourning process may be longer than that for death by natural causes.

Feeling sad is normal. Talk to your friends about how you feel and stay active with them. Talk to a school counselor about the loss of your friend.

IF YOU HELPED PREVENT THE SUICIDE

A person who was considering suicide may be angry with you for helping to prevent it. Up until the time of death, most suicidal people are undecided and wavering. They are really asking for help, although they won't admit it. Kelly was a popular girl who always planned to be a cheerleader. When she was told she had not made the squad and to wait till next year, she felt life was not worth living. She told several of her friends she did not want to live anymore. Her friend Tara thought she was kidding. Cordelia found the subject of suicide scary, so she put it out of her mind. Curran believed the old myth that people who talk about suicide never take action. When Kelly said she was dropping out of the "stupid school" that would not accept her as a cheerleader, she really meant she felt she did not belong there.

Kelly thought a lot about killing herself. The shame of not making the squad was bad enough, but then she would have to go to games and watch the girls who did. She could not bear this prospect. A friend who listened to her warnings of suicide led her to professional help. Although she would not speak to the friend for several weeks, later she realized that the friend had saved her life. Losing a friend for a few weeks is better than losing a friend forever.

A CALL TO ACTION

Many people do not recognize warnings about suicide. Many are also unaware that suicide is a major public health problem. Increased awareness about how to prevent suicide is one of the most important messages of the 1999 Surgeon General's Call to Action to Prevent Suicide. Wider public understanding of the science of the brain and behavior can reduce the stigma associated with seeking help for mental and substance abuse disorders and consequently may help reduce the risk for suicidal behavior.

Reduced stigma may lead to better reporting. Not all deaths that are suicides are reported as such. For example, deaths classified as homicides or accidents where individuals may have intentionally put themselves in harm's way are not included in suicide statistics. Secrecy and silence diminish the accuracy and amount of information available about persons who have completed suicide—information that might help prevent other suicides.

Many people do not realize that more teenagers and young adults die from suicide than from cancer, heart disease, AIDS, birth defects, pneumonia, influenza, and chronic lung disease combined.[10] Greater awareness of suicide as a public health problem may lead to the expansion of resources in communities for suicide prevention programs. Information about hotlines can be posted on bulletin boards where teenagers can be made aware of them. You can learn what to say and do in case you recognize a threat of suicide.

NOTES

1. Dr. Walter Menninger, Remarks at the Child Advocacy Conference, November 1, 1999.
   http://www.cdc.gov/safeusa/suicide.htm
2. http://www.nimh.nih.gov/publicat/harmaway.cfm
3. http://www.surgeongeneral.gov/library/calltoaction/fact3.htm
4. Nancy Merritt, "Teen and Young Adult Suicide," Tempe, AZ: Do It Now Foundation, #174, unpaged.

5. David Sachter, *Surgeon General's Call to Action to Prevent Suicide* (Washington, DC: U.S. Public Health Service, 1999).

6. http://www.suicidology.org/excerptpage2.htm

7. http://www.depression.com/health_library/types/types_04_major.html

8. Nancy Merritt, "Teen and Young Adult Suicide."

9. Ibid.

10. David Sachter, *Surgeon General's Call to Action*, p. 4.

Chapter Nine

RATE YOURSELF: CAN YOU TELL FACT FROM FICTION?

On a separate piece of paper, mark the numbers of the following statements as true of false. The answers are on page 99.

ABOUT DEPRESSION

1. Teenagers can't suffer from real depression.
2. Talking about depression or suicide makes it worse.
3. Telling an adult that a friend may be depressed is betraying a secret.
4. Depression will disappear on its own.
5. Symptoms of depression are easy to identify.
6. People should not be asked to "snap out" of depression.
7. Depression is a character flaw.
8. People who are depressed are tearful.
9. Antidepressant drugs are addicting.
10. Antidepressant drugs cause an artificial high or can change your personality.

ABOUT SUICIDE

1. People who talk about suicide don't take their lives.
2. The chances of suicide can be reduced by avoiding the subject.
3. There is no special type of person who commits suicide.
4. If a person is planning to kill himself or herself, no one can prevent it.
5. Talking about suicide may give someone the idea.

6. Suicide is a spontaneous act that happens without warning.

7. Telling people to cheer up will help to prevent suicide.

8. Most suicides are caused by events such as a broken love affair, rejection to a college of choice, or an argument with a parent.

9. People who commit suicide are people who are unwilling to seek help.

10. The suicide issue does not involve minorities.

ANSWERS ABOUT DEPRESSION

1. False

   Depression can affect people of any age. It is different from being moody.

2. False

   Asking about his or her wishes can help to make the person feel more understood and less trapped. Talking through feelings with a good friend can be a first step to getting help. Concern for and support of a friend can provide him or her with the encouragement to talk to an adult who can help the depressed person reach a doctor or therapist who can evaluate and treat the depression.

3. False

   Depression saps energy and self-esteem and can interfere with a person's wish or ability to get help. Sharing your concerns with an adult who can help is an act of friendship.

4. False

   Clinical depression is a serious illness that does not usually go away on its own. A combination of medication and counseling is the most effective help for most people. Not all depressed brains are the same, but untreated depression can cause years of needless pain for the depressed person and his or her family.

5. False

Depression can be disguised as another kind of problem. Emily was not satisfied when she looked in the mirror. She was very thin but she saw a fat girl there.

Emily was a teen who had an eating disorder known as anorexia nervosa. A typical meal consisted of an apple, a mushroom, and a cracker. When Emily's weight continued to fall, her grades fell. When her heart's rhythm grew abnormal, she found herself in the hospital with an intravenous tube supplying her calories. It never occurred to her or her parents that she was suffering from depression.

6. True

They may feel better day by day if they are treated for the illness.

7. False

Depression cannot be overcome by willpower. It is an illness, not a weakness or character flaw.

8. False

Many people who are depressed do not cry. Depression may be expressed in many ways, including meanness or anger.

9. False

Antidepressant drugs are not addicting.

10. False

Although antidepressants make a person feel better, they do not make one high or make changes in personality.

ANSWERS ABOUT SUICIDE

1. False

"You'll be sorry when I'm dead," "You won't have to worry about me tomorrow," may even be said jokingly but still give warning of a planned suicide. Many studies show that a large percentage of people who commit suicide communicated their intent before they died.

Statements about suicide may be warning signs. Families' feelings of guilt may play a part in forgetting such statements.

2. False

   Just the opposite is true. Knowing not to treat suicide as a taboo subject is one of the first steps toward prevention.

   The old attitude of hiding or denying suicide has been the cause of many unnecessary deaths. Consider the case of a young boy whose doctor was treating him for depression. The doctor recommended hospitalization because the boy appeared suicidal but the mother would not consider it because she was concerned about what her friends and neighbors would think. She refused to accept the idea that the boy might take his life.

   One afternoon, the boy sat in a rented hotel room for three hours with a gun sometimes pointed to his head. Finally, however, he put the gun in his pocket and returned home. His psychiatrist told the father about this incident, but the parents still would not consider hospitalization. They believed it was best not to talk about the subject. Two weeks later, the boy decided to punish his mother for nagging at him. He hanged himself in the basement while she was making dinner.

3. True

   A suicidal person may be rich, poor, young, old, a good or a bad student, or anything in between. Any person can be vulnerable.

4. Usually false

   Most suicidal people do not want to die. They want their pain to stop, and they may waver between life and death even until the very last minute. The impulse to commit suicide does not last forever. A mental health professional can help a person get through the worst times when the impulse seems overwhelming.

Statistics are not available for the number of suicides that have been prevented by calls to crisis centers, but there are hundreds of suicide prevention centers and an untold number of people are alive today because of them.

5. False

You will not make a person suicidal by talking about the subject. Just the opposite is true. Discussing the subject openly is one of the most helpful things one can do to prevent suicide.

6. False

Most suicidal people fantasize or plan their self-destruction long before making the attempt, but the act itself may be impulsive.[1] Most communicate their intent to friends, families, doctors, and others long before acting on it.

7. False

Telling a person to cheer up by pointing out good things in the future does not help a person who is experiencing the pain of deep depression now. This person cannot look much beyond the present. Telling the person what a good life he or she has only increases feelings of guilt.

8. False

Actually, many people have similar disappointments without ending their lives. The difference is depression.[2]

9. False

Studies of suicide victims show that more than half had sought medical help within six months of their deaths.[3]

10. False

Suicide rates are exploding for African American teens.

NOTES

1. Kay Redfield Jamison, *Night Falls Fast: Understanding Suicide* (New York: Knopf, 1999), p. 236.
2. http://www.suicidology.org/excerptpage2.htm
3. http://www.save.org/misconc.shtml

TO FIND OUT MORE

BOOKS

Appleton, William S. *Prozac and the New Antidepressants*. New York: Plume Books, Penguin Putnam, 2000.

Burns, David. *Feeling Good: The New Mood Therapy*. New York: Morrow/Avon, 1998.

Cobain, Bev. *When Nothing Matters Anymore: A Survival Guide for Depressed Teens*. Minneapolis, MN: Free Spirit Publishing, 1998.

Cronkite, Kathy. *On the Edge of Darkness: Conversations About Conquering Depression*. New York: Doubleday, 1994.

Fassler, David. *Help Me, I'm Sad: Recognizing, Treating and Preventing Childhood and Adolescent Depression*. New York: Penguin, 1998.

Fink, Max. *Electroshock: Restoring the Mind*. New York: Oxford University Press, 1999.

Garland, E. Jane. *Depression Is the Pits, But I'm Getting Better: A Guide for Adolescents*. Washington, DC: Magination Press, 1997.

Gootman, Marilyn. *When a Friend Dies: A Book for Teens About Grieving and Healing*. Minneapolis, MN: Free Spirit Publishing, 1994.

Hales, Robert E. and Dianne Hales. *The Mind/Mood Pill Book.* New York: Bantam Books, 2000.

Hyde, Margaret O. and Elizabeth H. Forsyth. *Know About Mental Illness.* New York: Walker, 1996.

———. *Suicide.* New York: Franklin Watts, 1997.

Irwin, Cait. *Conquering the Beast Within: How I Fought Depression and Won...and How You Can, Too.* New York: Times Books, 1999.

Jamison, Kay Redfield. *An Unquiet Mind: A Memoir of Moods and Madness.* New York: Alfred Knopf, 1995.

———. *Night Falls Fast: Understanding Suicide.* New York: Knopf, 1999.

———. *Touched with Fire: Manic-Depressive Illness and the Artistic Temperament.* New York: Free Press, 1996.

Levenkron, Steven. *Cutting: Understanding and Overcoming Self-Mutilation.* New York: W.W. Norton, 1995.

Nelson, Richard E. and Judith C. Galas. *The Power to Prevent Suicide.* Minneapolis, MN: Free Spirit Publishing, 1994.

Slaby, Andrew. *No One Saw My Pain: Why Teens Kill Themselves.* New York: W. W. Norton, 1996.

Smith, Judie. *Drugs and Suicide.* New York: Rosen Publishing Group, 1998.

Solomon, Andrew. *Noonday Demon: An Atlas of Depression.* New York: Scribner, 2001.

Stewart, Gail B. *Teens and Depression.* San Diego: Lucent Books, 1998.

Surgeon General's Call to Action to Prevent Suicide. Section Three, At a Glance: Suicide Among the Young. Washington, DC: Superintendent of Documents, 1999.
http://www.surgeongeneral.gov/library/calltoaction/fact3.htm

Winkler, Kathleen. *Teens, Depression, and the Blues: A Hot Issue*. Berkeley Heights, NJ: Enslow, 2000.

Wurtzel, Elizabeth. *Prozac Nation: Young and Depressed in America*. New York: Riverhead Books, 1995.

HELP WITH DEPRESSION

Depression, Recognition, Awareness and Treatment
1-800-421-4211 / 24 Hours (Automated System)
Operated by the National Institutes of Health
Leave name and address on machine to receive information on depression and anxiety disorders.

National Institute of Mental Health Information Center
1-301-443-453
Monday through Friday / 8:30-5:30 ET
Call this number to talk to someone about depression and its causes and treatments.
e-mail: nimhinfo@nih.gov
http://www.nimh.nih.gov/home.htm

HOTLINES FOR SUICIDE PREVENTION

Boy's Town National Hotline
1-800-448-3000 / 24 Hours
Operated by Boy's Town

National Suicide Hotline/National Hope Line Network
1-800-SUICIDE (784-2433) / 24 Hours
Operated by the American Association of Suicidology

National Youth Crisis Hotline
1-800-HIT HOME / 24 Hours
Operated by Children's Rights of America

Suicide and Crisis Hotline
1-800-999 9999 / 24 Hours
Operated by Covenant House

See the yellow pages of your local phone book for emergency phone numbers. Look under community services and suicide prevention. Local mobile crisis teams may be available in your area.

ORGANIZATIONS

American Association of Suicidology
4201 Connecticut Avenue NW, Suite 408
Washington, DC 20008
http://www.suicidology.org

American Foundation for Suicide Prevention
120 Wall Street, 22nd floor
New York, NY 10005
http://www.afsp.org

Depression and Related Affective Disorders (DRADA)
Meyer 3-181
600 North Wolfe Street
Baltimore, MD 21287
http://www.med.jhu.edu/drada

Joy's Famous People Files
http://www.frii/~parrot/living.html

National Alliance for the Mentally Ill
Colonial Place Three
2107 Wilson Blvd., Suite 300
Arlington, VA 22201
http://www.nami.org

National Depressive and Manic Depressive Association (NDMDA)
730 North Franklin Street
Suite 105
Chicago, IL 60610
1-800-826-3632
http://www.ndmda.org

National Foundation for Depressive Illness
P.O. Box 2257
New York, NY 10116-2257
http://www.depression.org

National Mental Health Association (NMHA)
1021 Prince Street
Alexandria, VA 22314-2971
www.nmha.org

National Mental Health Awareness Campaign
Toll-free help line: 1-877-495-0009
http://www.nostigma.org

Pendulum resources
http://www.pendulum.org

SA/VE—Suicide Awareness/Voices of Education
P.O. Box 24507
Minneapolis, MN 55424-0507
1-612-946-7998
http://www.save.org

GLOSSARY

Alzheimer's disease: progressive, irreversible brain disease that impairs memory, thinking, speech, recognition of familiar people or objects, judgment, and ability to perform ordinary tasks

antidepressants: medications that relieve depression by acting on certain neurotransmitters in the brain

attention deficit/hyperactivity disorder (ADHD): a condition characterized by impulsiveness and impaired attention span. Children are disruptive in class and may have learning difficulties.

auditory hallucination: the experience of hearing voices or other sounds that no one else hears; occurs without actual external stimulation

behavioral therapy: a form of psychotherapy that helps people learn new ways of behaving, solving problems, and relating to other people

circadian rhythms: biological rhythms with a cycle of twenty-four hours

clinical depression: a term used to describe serious depression

cognitive therapy: a short-term psychotherapy with a goal of changing negative, distorted thinking to positive thinking; an effective form of therapy for depression *cortisol*: hormone produced by the adrenal glands.

delusion: false, fixed belief not held by other people that has no basis in reality

dopamine: a neurotransmitter found in the brain. Low levels may be a cause of some kinds of depression.

dysphoria: feelings of unpleasantness, or a mood of dissatisfaction, sadness, anxiety, and irritability

dysthymic disorder (dysthymia): a mild, chronic form of depression that lasts at least two years in adults or one year in children

hypomania: a mild form of mania

lithium: a medication that controls both the high and low fluctuating moods of bipolar disorder

major depressive disorder (unipolar major depression): recurrent major depression without manic episode, as opposed to bipolar disorder

mania: a state of excessive elation characterized by increased energy, hyperactivity, racing thoughts, rapid talking, decreased need for sleep, poor judgment, inflated self-esteem, and inappropriate behavior

manic-depressive disorder (bipolar disorder): disorder characterized by alternating periods of mania and depression; also known as manic depression

masked depression: a type of depression in which usual symptoms are hidden behind a variety of other psychological or physical symptoms

melatonin: hormone involved in regulation of biological rhythms

monoamine oxide inhibitor (MAOI): a type of antidepressant

mood reactivity: capacity of a depressed individual to cheer up when something positive happens; characteristic of atypical depression

neuron: a nerve cell

neurotransmitter: a chemical that carries a message across gaps between neurons. An imbalance of neurotransmitters has been linked to depression.

norepinephrine: one of the three major neurotransmitters found in the brain

postpartum depression: a form of depression associated with childbirth

psychodynamic therapy: therapy that explores the mind for unresolved conflicts

psychosis: impairment of ability to recognize reality. For example, a person who has delusions or hallucinations is psychotic.

selective serotonin reuptake inhibitors (SSRIs): a group of antidepressants that work by blocking the reabsorption of serotonin in the brain, raising the level of this neurotransmitter

serotonin: one of three major neurotransmitters found in synapses between neurons that is linked to depression

synapse: the gap between two neurons at which the transmission of messages occurs

tricyclic antidepressant: a class of antidepressants that increase the amount of norepinephrine and serotonin in the synapses in the brain

INDEX